Diseases and Disorders of Youth

Kids and ADHD

Melissa Abramovitz

ReferencePoint Press®

San Diego, CA

About the Author

Melissa Abramovitz is an award-winning author/freelance writer who specializes in writing educational nonfiction books and magazine articles for all age groups, from preschoolers through adults. She has published hundreds of magazine articles and more than fifty educational books for children and teenagers. She also does freelance editing and writes short stories, poems, picture books, and materials for authors. Abramovitz graduated *summa cum laude* from the University of California, San Diego, with a degree in psychology and is also a graduate of the Institute of Children's Literature.

For more information, contact:
ReferencePoint Press, Inc.
PO Box 27779
San Diego, CA 92198
www.ReferencePointPress.com

LIBRARY OF CONGRESS CATALOGING-IN-PUBLICATION DATA

Names: Abramovitz, Melissa, 1954– author.
Title: Kids and ADHD/by Melissa Abramovitz.
Description: San Diego, CA: ReferencePoint Press, Inc., 2019. | Series: Diseases and Disorders of Youth | Audience: Diseases and Disorders of Youth | Includes bibliographical references and index.
Identifiers: LCCN 2018022048 (print) | LCCN 2018022228 (ebook) | ISBN 9781682823927 (eBook) | ISBN 9781682823910 (hardback)
Subjects: LCSH: Attention-deficit-disordered children—Juvenile literature.
Classification: LCC RJ506.H9 (ebook) | LCC RJ506.H9 A3377 2019 (print) | DDC 618.92/8589—dc23
LC record available at https://lccn.loc.gov/2018022048

Contents

The Most Commonly Diagnosed Disorder in Kids

People with attention-deficit/hyperactivity disorder (ADHD) have trouble paying attention and controlling emotions and behavior. According to the Centers for Disease Control and Prevention (CDC), ADHD is the most commonly diagnosed chronic (long-lasting) psychiatric disorder in kids. The number of diagnoses in children and teenagers rose steadily during the late twentieth and early twenty-first centuries, climbing from 3.3 million in 1997 to 5 million in 2009 and eventually to 6.1 million in 2016.

Why the Increases?

However, experts are not sure whether more children are developing ADHD or whether other factors are increasing the number of diagnoses. Child psychologist Tiffany R. Farchione thinks the increase "might be because of greater public awareness of the disorder and psychiatric illnesses in general."[1] On the other hand, psychologist Stephen Hinshaw and health economist Richard Scheffler attribute the increase to school funding issues. Their research shows that US states with the most ADHD diagnoses have laws that tie school funding to the number of students who pass standardized tests. Schools in these states encourage parents of struggling students to seek an ADHD diagnosis and a prescription for ADHD drugs to help children settle down so they can do better on tests. Indeed, CDC data shows that 13 percent of the children in Kentucky, which has such laws, were diagnosed with ADHD, compared to 3.8 percent in Nevada, which does not. As Hinshaw explains, "The diagnosis depends on behavior. We don't have a laboratory test, so diagnosis is always going to have a subjective component: Does this child's behavior fit into this classroom, or fit into this family, or this culture?"[2]

> "The diagnosis depends on behavior. We don't have a laboratory test, so diagnosis is always going to have a subjective component: Does this child's behavior fit into this classroom, or fit into this family, or this culture?"[2]
>
> —Psychologist Stephen Hinshaw

Others, like investigative journalist Alan Schwarz, believe aggressive marketing of ADHD drugs by pharmaceutical companies, along with parents and teachers looking for quick ways to calm boisterous children, has led to widespread overdiagnosis and misdiagnosis. Schwarz calls ADHD "the most misdiagnosed condition in American medicine"[3] in his 2016 book *ADHD Nation.* He notes that his investigation revealed that parents and teachers commonly pressure doctors to diagnose ADHD in normal, active children who are somewhat disruptive. He cites instances in which teachers and school administrators tell parents that their disruptive children can no longer attend school unless they start taking ADHD drugs, regardless of whether they actually have the disorder. This practice has become so common that child

> "[ADHD is] the most misdiagnosed condition in American medicine."[3]
>
> —Investigative journalist Alan Schwarz

psychiatrist Peter Breggin, another critic of ADHD overdiagnosis, stated on national television, "These drugs alleviate the suffering of *teachers* in overcrowded classrooms"[4] by calming rowdy kids who have no need for medication.

A Social Issue

Whatever the reasons for increased diagnoses, the prevalence of ADHD has made it a social problem as well as a condition that challenges individuals and families. The CDC notes that ADHD-associated costs, estimated to total $38 billion to $72 billion each year, constitute the second-highest source of health-related costs for children in the United States. Taxpayers cover the medical costs of low-income families and the costs of special education

People with ADHD have trouble paying attention, and controlling emotions and behavior. Kids with ADHD struggle with school and social interaction.

that all children with a disability are entitled to receive in public schools. Children and teens with ADHD are at high risk for risky and delinquent behavior, and taxpayers also cover any costs related to law enforcement and juvenile justice.

The costs related to special education programs are especially significant because schools must provide every child who has a disability with an individualized education plan (IEP), special education teachers, and counseling and/or specialized therapy, such as anger management therapy, if needed. According to the ADHD support organization Children and Adults with Attention-Deficit/Hyperactivity Disorder (CHADD), education-related expenses for children with ADHD cost taxpayers anywhere from approximately $2,000 to $12,000 per child per year, depending on age, ADHD severity, and necessary therapies.

The costs for families who have private health insurance are also high. A 2017 survey by *ADDitude* magazine found that such families commonly spend from $2,000 to more than $5,000 per year for expenses that exceed those covered by insurance. Twenty-three percent of the survey respondents said they could not afford these expenses, so their children with ADHD received no treatment. One parent stated, "Taking care of my kids properly should not cost more than my monthly house payment."[5]

Other Social Issues

Despite the expenditures, kids with ADHD tend to do poorly in school and struggle socially. Those who receive treatment do better than others, but many are not diagnosed or treated until they are already lagging behind in school (often between the ages of eight and ten), and they cannot catch up. Poor school performance, along with having few or no friends because of their behavior, contributes to other social concerns.

For one thing, frustration about poor grades and having few friends feeds the tendency for adolescents with ADHD to drop out of school and/or engage in risky behaviors that affect individuals, families, and society. For example, the CDC states that 35 percent of American teens with ADHD drop out of school, compared with around 10 percent of their peers. Teens with ADHD are also two and a half times more likely than their peers to be expelled from school and two to four times more likely to cause traffic accidents.

The prevalence of ADHD has resulted in increased efforts to help kids with the disorder succeed in school and in life. More and more of them are able to build on help they receive from tutors and special education programs to go to college; in fact, so many teens with ADHD now go to college that many of these institutions have implemented special ADHD services and accommodations. Some offer special orientation programs, tutoring, ADHD counselors, personal coaches to check in with daily, special arrangements for taking tests, and note takers to help out in class. This allows many college-aged people with ADHD to comfortably leave home and start to manage the disorder on their own as they enter adulthood. As the number of ADHD diagnoses continues to climb, schools at all levels and society in general are adapting to make life easier and more fulfilling for those living with the disorder.

Chapter 1

What Is ADHD?

ADHD is a brain disorder that starts during childhood and often persists into adolescence and sometimes into adulthood. Overall, the CDC says 5 to 10 percent of children and 3 to 5 percent of American adults have ADHD. Its main hallmark is a lack of control of self-regulation. This means that people with ADHD have trouble paying attention and controlling certain emotions, such as anger. They are also likely to act on impulse and to be hyperactive, meaning that they are constantly in motion and tend to talk nonstop.

Although ADHD is often defined by specific symptoms, including hyperactivity, experts emphasize that it is more than a collection of symptoms. "*There's a lot more to ADHD than inattention and hyperactivity,*" writes ADHD expert Joel T. Nigg in his book *Getting Ahead of ADHD*. "The broader capacity of *self-regulation* is much more at the core of ADHD than these individual symptoms."[6]

The ability to self-regulate, in turn, involves an important mental capability called executive function. Executive function refers to brain activities that allow an individual to manage and organize the ways in which he or she gets things done. The relationship between executive function and self-regulation is complex, and different experts define these terms in different ways. Nigg defines *self-regulation* as "similar to executive functioning but broader, . . . the capacity to optimize our behavior, thinking and attention, and emotional experience and expression."[7] Psychologists Roy F. Baumeister, Brandon J. Schmeichel, and Kathleen D. Vohs simplify this relationship by explaining that "self-regulation is one of the self's major executive functions."[8]

Clinical psychologist Thomas E. Brown likens executive function in the brain to the conductor of an orchestra: "The conductor organizes, activates, focuses, integrates, and directs the musicians as they play. Similarly, the brain's executive functions organize, activate, focus, integrate and direct, allowing the brain to perform both routine and creative work."[9] The deficiencies in executive function and self-regulation found in people with ADHD therefore affect an individual's ability to focus, think, and control and organize thoughts and behavior.

Not a New Disorder

The lack of self-regulation and the characteristic symptoms seen in children with ADHD have appeared in references dating to 1798, even though the disorder was not referred to as ADHD until 1987. Historians attribute the first-known formal description of an ADHD-like disorder to the Scottish physician Sir Alexander Crichton. In 1798 Crichton wrote that "the barking of dogs, an ill-tuned organ, or the scolding of women, are sufficient to distract patients of this description to such a degree, as almost approaches to the nature of delirium." He also noted that the disorder had adverse effects on an individual's ability to learn, "inasmuch as it renders him incapable of attending with constancy to any one object of education." These characteristics are consistent with modern descriptions of ADHD. However, twenty-first-century experts know that Crichton's observation that the disorder "is generally diminished with age"[10] is often untrue. The CDC states that ADHD is a lifelong disease in more than half of all cases.

How Many Young People Have ADHD?

The number of children and teenagers diagnosed with ADHD has changed over time, according to CDC data that comes from the National Survey of Children's Health and other sources. The CDC report shows that 6.1 million young people, or about 9.4 percent of youth between the ages of two and seventeen, had ever been diagnosed with ADHD.

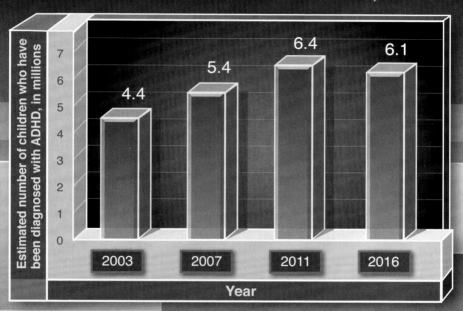

Estimated Number of Children Who Ever Had ADHD, in Millions

Note: Due to changes in methodology, 2016 numbers are based on an age range of two to seventeen; statistics for previous years are based on an age range of four to seventeen.

Source: Centers for Disease Control and Prevention, "Attention-Deficit/Hyperactivity Disorder (ADHD): Data & Statistics," 2018. www.cdc.gov.

Another well-known early reference to an ADHD-like disorder appears in a children's book titled *Struwwelpeter*, written by the German psychiatrist Heinrich Hoffmann in 1846. One story in the book, "Fidgety Phil," was about a boy named Philipp who constantly fidgets and displays inattention and hyperactivity. In the story, Philipp's father asks him to sit still at the dinner table, "but Philipp did not listen to what the father was saying to him. . . . [He] wriggled and giggled, and then, I declare, swung backward

Is ADHD a Real Disease?

Some experts, including behavioral neurologist Richard Saul, believe ADHD is a catchall label for difficult children and is not a real disease. In his 2014 book *ADHD Does Not Exist,* Saul writes that many children diagnosed with ADHD actually have another disorder, such as anxiety, depression, or oppositional defiant disorder. "Once I treated what I saw as the primary diagnosis . . . the attention-deficit and hyperactivity symptoms usually disappeared, leading me to believe that . . . the symptoms of ADHD are better explained by other conditions. In other words, ADHD, as we currently define it, does not exist," he explains.

Other experts argue that brain abnormalities in people with ADHD prove it is a distinct and real disorder. In 2017 geneticist Martine Hoogman and her colleagues at Radboud University Medical Center in the Netherlands published a study that found five areas in the brain are abnormally small and underdeveloped in children with ADHD. These areas regulate attention, learning, memory, emotions, and self-control, which are all deficient in people with ADHD. "The results from our study confirm that people with ADHD have differences in their brain structure and therefore suggest ADHD is a disorder of the brain. We hope that this will help reduce stigma that ADHD is 'just a label' for difficult children," states Hoogman. Other studies have found that the prefrontal cortex (part of the cerebral cortex, or the "thinking" part of the brain) in children with ADHD is also smaller than normal.

Richard Saul, *ADHD Does Not Exist.* New York: HarperCollins, 2014, pp. xvii, xvi.

Quoted in Melissa Jenco, "Study: Brain Differences Found in children with ADHD," AAP News, February 16, 2017. www .aappublications.org.

and forward and tilted his chair."[11] Philipp's chair then falls over, dragging dishes and food off the table, and his parents become angry. The entire scenario is consistent with the characteristics and family conflicts that occur in households with ADHD.

Despite these early descriptions, doctors did not consider ADHD-like behavior to constitute a specific mental disorder until the 1900s. Many medical historians consider a series of lectures called the Goulstonian Lectures, given by the British pediatrician Sir George Frederic Still in 1902, to represent the beginning of the history of ADHD as a clearly defined medical disorder. Still described a group of forty-three children with hyperactivity, problems paying and sustaining attention, and problems regulating emotion and behavior. The children also tended to be aggressive, defiant, spiteful, and resistant to discipline. Still attributed these behaviors to a "defect of moral consciousness" that led to a lack "of moral control." He further noted that these children did not learn from the consequences of their actions, even though they were "without general impairment of intellect." Indeed, he noted that most were of normal intelligence, which is typical of children with ADHD. However, experts believe Still's descriptions were of children who had an ADHD-like illness combined with another mental disorder that may have been either what is now known as oppositional defiant disorder or conduct disorder. This is because children with ADHD are not usually spiteful, and even though they often resist the effects of punishment, they are not morally deficient. In any case, Still referred to the disorder he described as "an abnormal psychical condition in children."[12]

In 1932 the German physicians Franz Kramer and Hans Pollnow referred to an ADHD-like disorder as "a hyperkinetic disease of infancy."[13] According to psychologists at the University of Regensburg in Germany, Kramer and Pollnow described affected children who "indiscriminately touch or move everything available without pursuing a goal. . . . These children switch the light on and off, move chairs around the room, climb the table, the cupboard or the windowsill, jump around in their beds, turn keys in the keyhole, go round in circles."[14] This emphasis on the hyperactivity aspects of the disorder persisted for the next several decades; in 1957 psychiatrists officially named it *hyperkinetic impulse disorder*.

However, numerous experts pointed out that the severity and nature of symptoms varied among individuals, and some thought

> "These children switch the light on and off, move chairs around the room, climb the table, the cupboard or the windowsill, jump around in their beds, turn keys in the keyhole, go round in circles."[14]
>
> —Neuropsychologist Klaus W. Lange and colleagues paraphrasing German physicians Franz Kramer and Hans Pollnow

the diverse symptoms of hyperactivity, inattention, and impulsivity should be united under a new name that alluded to the common characteristic of minimal brain damage. Based on this viewpoint, a task force convened by the National Institute of Neurological Diseases and Blindness during the early 1960s recommended calling the disease *minimal brain dysfunction syndrome*. Psychiatry and pediatrics professor Sam D. Clements wrote a description of the syndrome based on the task force's findings, explaining that it affected "children of near average, average, or above average general intelligence with certain learning or behavioral disabilities ranging from mild to severe" and involved "impairment in perception, conceptualization, language, memory, and control of attention, impulse, or motor function."[15]

Critics claimed the label of minimal brain dysfunction was too general and vague to be useful, and many insisted that the name should include the word *hyperactivity*. Based on these sentiments, in 1968 the American Psychiatric Association used the name *hyperkinetic reaction of childhood* in the second edition of the *Diagnostic and Statistical Manual* that it publishes to help psychiatrists diagnose and treat mental disorders. But again, experts argued over whether inattention and impulsivity were also hallmark characteristics. In 1980 the American Psychiatric Association renamed it *attention deficit disorder with or without hyperactivity*. In 1987 the American Psychiatric Association renamed it *ADHD*, and in 1994 it subdivided ADHD into the three subtypes that are still used in diagnosis: predominantly inattentive presentation, predominantly hyperactive-impulsive presentation, and combined presentation.

The Characteristics of ADHD

The name *ADHD* reflects the most prominent behaviors that derive from an individual's lack of self-regulation. However, inattention, hyperactivity, and impulsivity are not the only characteristic behaviors seen in children with the disorder. Kids with ADHD also have trouble controlling their emotions, and in many cases they display what experts call hyperfocus. This refers to the fact that they can pay attention to things they find interesting, such as a favorite video game, for hours.

Other common behaviors in kids with ADHD include not doing what parents or teachers instruct them to do and not remembering things. In some cases, if a parent tells the child to stop banging on a table, he may stop for a minute and then resume the behavior because he forgets what he was told. Other children do not complete tasks like homework because their attention flits from one thing to another. Kids with ADHD also frequently lose things. One mother commented that her son lost his lunchbox nearly every day at school because he would put it down, start doing something else, and completely forget about the lunchbox. The inability to focus and stick with one thing is one factor that accounts for the difficulties kids with ADHD have with learning and doing well in school. Because of these difficulties, some experts have suggested that ADHD should be classified as a learning disability.

Many young people with ADHD display what experts call hyperfocus. This refers to their ability to focus for hours on things they find interesting, such as a favorite video game.

However, others point out that ADHD affects far more aspects of existence than learning, so it is not classified in this way. As the ADHD support organization Understand explains, "ADHD isn't a learning disability, even though it can affect learning."[16]

The inattention that affects learning often does not become obvious until a child starts school, but the restlessness and hyperactivity seen in kids with ADHD often appears very early on. Many infants with ADHD sleep little and are fussy and restless. They tend to also have feeding problems and bouts of unexplained crying. Once a baby with ADHD starts walking, he is likely to run around destroying or climbing on everything in sight. Stories about children with ADHD climbing onto the top of the refrigerator or trying to jump from a second-story window are common. Many parents of toddlers and young children with ADHD say their child "acts as if driven by a motor,"[17] according to CHADD.

Once a child starts school, hyperactivity often makes it impossible for him or her to stay seated in situations where sitting still is expected. For example, Sarah, a young adult with ADHD, describes how hyperactivity affected her as a child: "I remember being in class and feeling like I was going to explode if I couldn't get out of my seat,"[18] she explains. She would then ask to go to the restroom, and she would spend hours running up and down staircases instead of returning to class. Many kids with hyperactivity also tend to talk nonstop, including interrupting others and whining or screaming to direct attention to themselves.

The impulsivity in ADHD often becomes more pronounced as a child grows. A seven-year-old boy named Dan, for instance, knocked down a stack of blocks a child near him had built on a table without stopping to consider that this was not a kind thing to do. Older children with ADHD typically do impulsive things like driving a car around a curve at breakneck speed because it looks like fun. Closely related to impulsivity is the fact that kids with ADHD want what they want immediately and are not willing to wait. If parents or others refuse to give them what they want, they will often fly into a rage and have a tantrum.

Objective Criteria for Diagnosis

Since an ADHD diagnosis depends on the subjective opinions of parents, teachers, and doctors, experts believe it is important to develop objective diagnostic tests. As of 2018, no such tests were available. But research suggests that measuring brain waves (electrical activity in the brain) may someday be used as an objective diagnostic criterion.

Researchers measure brain waves by placing electrodes on the scalp. Scientists at the University of California, Davis, Mind Institute measured two types of brain waves—alpha and beta—while teenagers with and without ADHD performed a series of tasks on a computer. Alpha waves appear when someone is processing incoming sensory information, and beta waves occur during the performance of motor tasks. Some of the teens with ADHD had the inattentive subtype, and others had the combined subtype.

The researchers found that the brain waves of teens with both types of ADHD differed from those in kids without ADHD. However, those with inattentive ADHD showed differences in their alpha wave patterns, but those with the combined type showed differences in their beta waves. Researcher Catherine Fassbender explains that those with inattentive ADHD "had problems processing the cues" on the computer screen that were helping them perform the task, "whereas [those with] the combined type had problems using the cues to prepare a motor response" that consisted of pushing a button. Fassbender notes that analyzing differences in brain waves might someday lead to objective methods of diagnosing ADHD and of allowing doctors to distinguish different ADHD subtypes.

Quoted in UC Davis Mind Institute, "Scott Adams: Living with ADHD," *ADHD News*, Winter 2013/2014. www.ucdmc .ucdavis.edu.

Although ADHD is likely to last a lifetime, in many people certain symptoms lessen with time. Some kids are hyperactive as toddlers and display more inattention in elementary school and beyond. In some, impulsivity may not become pronounced until adolescence, when taking risks and engaging in impulsive behaviors is common. But in others, impulsivity diminishes during adolescence.

Diagnosing ADHD

Diagnosing ADHD can be challenging because of the wide range of behaviors present in children with the disorder. There are also no imaging, blood, or other laboratory tests that can be used in diagnosis. A medical doctor, often a pediatrician or psychiatrist, or a psychologist diagnoses ADHD on the basis of a child's symptoms, a physical exam to rule out other medical problems, clinical interviews with the child and his parents and teachers, and standardized rating scales. Experts say ADHD cannot be formally diagnosed in children under age four, but many parents who are concerned about a child under four may still have the child evaluated. Most children are diagnosed in elementary school; the CDC states that the average age at diagnosis is seven. Clinicians sometimes diagnose ADHD in adolescents or adults, but they only do so if symptoms were present before age twelve.

The current edition of the *Diagnostic and Statistical Manual (DSM-5)* includes criteria for diagnosing the inattention aspects of the disorder in children aged sixteen or younger. These include six or more symptoms of inattention that are present for at least six months. Five or more such symptoms must be present for at least six months to diagnose an adolescent aged seventeen or older or an adult with ADHD. The *DSM-5* lists the following symptoms for diagnosing inattention:

- Often fails to give close attention to details or makes careless mistakes in schoolwork, at work, or with other activities.
- Often has trouble holding attention on tasks or play activities.
- Often does not seem to listen when spoken to directly.
- Often does not follow through on instructions and fails to finish schoolwork, chores, or duties in the workplace (e.g., loses focus, side-tracked).
- Often has trouble organizing tasks and activities.

- Often avoids, dislikes, or is reluctant to do tasks that require mental effort over a long period of time (such as schoolwork or homework).
- Often loses things necessary for tasks and activities (e.g. school materials, pencils, books, tools, wallets, keys, paperwork, eyeglasses, mobile telephones).
- Is often easily distracted.
- Is often forgetful in daily activities.[19]

Diagnosing the hyperactivity and impulsivity aspects of the disorder requires identifying six or more symptoms of hyperactivity and impulsivity for children up to age sixteen or five or more for teens age seventeen and older and adults. These symptoms must have been present for at least six months and must be disruptive and inappropriate for the person's developmental level. The *DSM-5* lists these symptoms of hyperactivity and impulsivity:

- Often fidgets with or taps hands or feet, or squirms in seat.
- Often leaves seat in situations when remaining seated is expected.
- Often runs about or climbs in situations where it is not appropriate (adolescents or adults may be limited to feeling restless).
- Often unable to play or take part in leisure activities quietly.
- Is often "on the go" acting as if "driven by a motor."
- Often talks excessively.
- Often blurts out an answer before a question has been completed.
- Often has trouble waiting his/her turn.
- Often interrupts or intrudes on others (e.g., butts into conversations or games).[20]

The *DSM-5* also requires these conditions to be present:

- Several inattentive or hyperactive-impulsive symptoms were present before age 12 years.

- Several symptoms are present in two or more settings (such as at home, school or work; with friends or relatives; in other activities).

- There is clear evidence that the symptoms interfere with, or reduce the quality of, social, school, or work functioning.

- The symptoms are not better explained by another mental disorder (such as a mood disorder, anxiety disorder, dissociative disorder, or a personality disorder).[21]

These criteria make it clear that symptoms and behaviors used to diagnose ADHD must be ongoing, must have a noticeable impact on everyday functioning, and must be inappropriate for the person's developmental age. As psychiatrist Benedetto Vitiello of the National Institutes of Health explains, "The diagnosis is made because the level of hyperactivity or lack of concentration is extreme and prevents the child from engaging in what would be expected activities appropriate to their development."[22] For instance, seventeen-year-old Max's parents state that he constantly climbs on statues or other structures when he and his family walk around town—like many three- to seven-year-olds typically do. This makes it difficult for Max to fit in with his peers in high school. However, if Max were four years old and behaved this way, his behavior would not qualify him for an ADHD diagnosis unless it was extreme.

> "The diagnosis is made because the level of hyperactivity or lack of concentration is extreme and prevents the child from engaging in what would be expected activities appropriate to their development."[22]
>
> —Psychiatrist Benedetto Vitiello of the National Institutes of Health

ADHD is three times more common in boys than girls. However, girls are more likely than boys to have the inattentive type of ADHD.

Doctors also use standardized rating scales when diagnosing ADHD. The most commonly used scales are the Conners Comprehensive Behavior Rating Scales developed by psychologist C. Keith Conners during the 1960s. Conners is considered to be the father of ADHD diagnosis since he devised these scales, which contain different questionnaires for parents, teachers, and children. Questions center on perceptions of a child's emotions, behaviors, and academic and social difficulties by the child, parents, and teachers. Psychologists convert scores obtained through the questionnaires to standardized scores called T-scores, and these T-scores can then be used to diagnose the type and severity of ADHD.

The Types of ADHD

Doctors can diagnose three subtypes, or presentations, of ADHD. *Combined presentation* is diagnosed if enough symptoms of both inattention and hyperactivity-impulsivity have been present for six months. *Predominantly inattentive presentation* is diagnosed if enough symptoms of inattention, but not hyperactivity-impulsivity, are present for six months. *Predominantly hyperactive-impulsive presentation* is diagnosed if enough symptoms of hyperactivity-impulsivity, but not inattention, are present for six months. Along with diagnosing a subtype, physicians determine whether a case is mild, moderate, or severe. In 2016, 14.5 percent of children diagnosed with ADHD had a severe case, 43.7 percent had moderate ADHD, and 41.8 percent had mild ADHD.

Both boys and girls are diagnosed with the subtypes of ADHD, but girls are more likely to have the inattentive type, and boys are more likely to have hyperactivity and impulsivity. Overall, the CDC states that ADHD is three times more common in boys than in girls. But the American Academy of Pediatrics emphasizes that ADHD is in no way just a boy's disease: "More girls than boys qualify for the diagnosis of ADHD, but more girls remain undiagnosed because they have the inattentive type of ADHD, and tend to be overlooked entirely or do not attract attention until they are older."[23] This is because a child who daydreams or fails to pay attention is not usually disruptive, unlike kids who display hyperactivity and impulsivity.

> "More girls than boys qualify for the diagnosis of ADHD, but more girls remain undiagnosed because they have the inattentive type of ADHD, and tend to be overlooked entirely or do not attract attention until they are older."[23]
>
> —The American Academy of Pediatrics

The Difficulties in Diagnosis

Diagnosing ADHD without completely objective criteria is difficult for several reasons. First of all, most children display behaviors that are similar to ADHD symptoms at some time; every child can be inattentive, hyperactive, or impulsive on occasion. But as psychiatrists Paul H. Wender and David A. Tomb explain in their book *ADHD*, these behaviors themselves do not constitute a diagnosable disorder unless they are excessive, long-term, and profoundly affect everyday functioning. "What characterizes ADHD children is the *intensity*, the *persistence*, and the *patterning* of these symptoms,"[24] they write.

Diagnosis is also complicated by the fact that 25 to 40 percent of kids with ADHD also have learning disorders such as dyslexia, which makes it difficult to read; 40 to 50 percent also have oppositional defiant disorder, characterized by anger, defiance, and vindictiveness; and 15 percent also have conduct disorder, characterized by cruelty to animals and people, aggressiveness, and criminal behavior. These disorders share some characteristics with ADHD, and the overlap of symptoms can make it difficult to distinguish them from ADHD.

Some medical conditions also share symptoms with ADHD, and a case involving a nine-year-old named Cecil illustrates the importance of considering all possibilities before making a diagnosis. Cecil had difficulties focusing in school and was especially reluctant to read. His teachers suspected he had ADHD or a learning disability. But a psychologist who evaluated Cecil noticed that Cecil's eyes did not move together when he looked at things around him. She recommended a visit to an ophthalmologist, a medical doctor who specializes in diagnosing and treating eye diseases. The ophthalmologist found that eye muscle problems prevented Cecil from coordinating movement and vision between both eyes. He prescribed special glasses and exercises, and suddenly Cecil's reading and attention problems disappeared. Had the psychologist who evaluated Cecil not looked beyond a possible ADHD diagnosis, Cecil might have received improper treatment and been given a label that could affect him for a lifetime.

Cases like Cecil's highlight the reasons that ADHD experts hope objective tests will be developed for diagnosing the disorder. Such tests could involve measurable substances in the blood, measurable structural brain differences in people with and without ADHD, or measurable differences in brain waves. Such criteria would vastly reduce the number of cases that are misdiagnosed for technical, social, or political reasons.

Chapter 2

What Causes ADHD?

ADHD is caused by defects in the development and wiring of the brain. These defects are in turn caused by complex interactions between a genetic predisposition, environmental influences, and early life experiences.

Genetic Factors

The role of genes in causing ADHD is shown by the fact that ADHD tends to run in families. Children whose parents or siblings have ADHD are at higher risk for the disorder than others. People with no family members who have ADHD have a 4 to 6 percent chance of developing it, but a child who has a parent with ADHD has up to a 50 percent chance of having the disorder. The sibling of a child with ADHD has a 25 to 30 percent chance of also having the disorder, and if one identical twin has ADHD, the other twin has an 80 percent chance of having it. Fraternal twins have the same risk of both having ADHD as other siblings.

Since most children live with their biological parents and siblings, it is possible that the increased risk for ADHD comes from living in a common environment as well as from sharing certain genes. To compare the effects of genes and environment, scientists study the prevalence of ADHD in children reared by adoptive parents. These studies show that adopted children are likely to develop ADHD if their biological parents are affected, confirming the strong influence of genes in causing the disorder.

Some diseases, such as cystic fibrosis, are caused by abnormalities, or mutations, in a single gene. People who inherit this gene invariably develop the disease. But the tendency to develop ADHD comes from mutations in many genes. An individual with these mutations will not develop ADHD unless certain environmental factors or experiences are also present. As psychologist Joel T. Nigg explains, when multiple genes affect susceptibility to a disorder, "genes aren't destiny; rather, they affect probability."[25]

Which Genes?

Researchers have identified close to fifty genes that play a role in causing ADHD. According to ADHD expert Russell Barkley, "The more of these genes you have, the higher the risk of getting ADHD and the increased odds that the condition will be more severe."[26]

One such gene mutation is in the serotonin transporter gene. This gene regulates the reuptake of the neurotransmitter (chemical messenger) serotonin, which plays a role in mood, memory, alertness, and behavior. After a neuron (nerve cell) releases a neurotransmitter to communicate with other neurons, the substance crosses a tiny gap between neurons called a synapse. Receptors on neighboring neurons take up the neurotransmitter, and the sending neuron soaks up whatever is left in the synapse in a process called reuptake. Reuptake allows the neuron to quickly resume communications. According to psychologist Thomas E. Brown, "In one millisecond, one thousandth of a second, twelve

> "The more of these genes you have, the higher the risk of getting ADHD and the increased odds that the condition will be more severe."[26]
>
> —Clinical psychologist and ADHD expert Russell Barkley

messages can be carried across the synaptic gap."[27] Mutations in the serotonin transporter gene interfere with this process, resulting in abnormally low amounts of serotonin in certain areas of the brain. Scientists have found that this contributes to upsetting the delicate balance of serotonin and a neurotransmitter called dopamine in these areas, and this is one factor that increases the risk for ADHD.

Researchers have also tied a specific mutation in the *DAT1* gene, which regulates dopamine transporters in the brain, to ADHD. The mutation leads cells to produce too many dopamine transporters, which suck up dopamine before it attaches to dopamine receptors on neurons in areas of the brain, such as the prefrontal cortex, linked to ADHD. Low levels of dopamine in these areas lead to difficulties with attention, learning, motivation, emotional control, and other aspects of executive function.

Another gene mutation linked to ADHD shows how the dopamine and/or serotonin deficiencies that underlie the disorder can result from diverse processes. This mutation is in the meth-

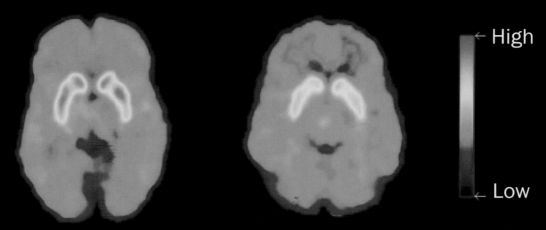

This image compares brain scans of a control subject (left) and an ADHD subject (right) with dopamine transporters indicated in orange. The ADHD brain delivers much lower levels of dopamine than the control brain.

High

Low

Control Subject   ADHD Subject

ylenetetrahydrofolate reductase (*MTHFR*) gene, which instructs the body how to manufacture an enzyme of the same name, the *MTHFR* enzyme. This enzyme is needed to process folate, also known as folic acid or vitamin B9. Normally, the *MTHFR* enzyme converts folate to a form called methylfolate. In this form it is capable of converting amino acids, which are the building blocks of proteins, into dopamine and serotonin. But a mutated *MTHFR* gene does not produce enough *MTHFR* enzyme to manufacture normal amounts of dopamine and serotonin, and these deficiencies can lead to ADHD.

Another job the *MTHFR* gene does is code for chemicals that break down heavy metals such as lead and other minerals that get into the body. When levels of these substances rise, hyperactivity often results. This is another way in which *MTHFR* mutations can contribute to ADHD.

Environment and Experience

None of the many genetic mutations that can contribute to causing ADHD is sufficient to produce the disorder on its own. These gene abnormalities make an individual more susceptible to ADHD, but certain events must also occur in a child's environment or experience. These events must damage areas of the brain that control executive function. One common source of this damage is exposure to toxins such as lead, pesticides, cigarette smoke, or alcohol before or after birth. Lead is a known neurotoxin, which is a poison that damages the brain. It was banned for use in paint in 1976 and in gasoline in 1990 in the United States, but older buildings may still contain leaded paint. Brain damage can result if a child touches or breathes lead dust or eats paint chips.

Pesticides are commonly sprayed in homes and schools to control bugs, and these chemicals are also linked to a variety of brain disorders, including ADHD. Similar effects can result from exposure to cigarette smoke or alcohol when a pregnant mother smokes or drinks or when someone smokes near a child later on.

Other events that can trigger ADHD in genetically susceptible children are prolonged stress or prolonged labor in a pregnant mother, low birth weight, and premature birth. In fact, a study published in 2017 by researchers at the Federal University of Rio Grande do Sul in Brazil found that babies who are underweight at birth or are born prematurely are three times more likely to develop ADHD than full-term infants or those born at a healthy weight.

Another factor that often triggers ADHD is oxygen deprivation during or after birth. Doctors have been aware of this for many years. In a study of seven hundred children with ADHD-like symptoms in 1948, doctors George Rosenfeld and Charles Bradley at the Emma Pendleton Bradley Home for kids with behavior problems found that children who suffered oxygen deprivation from birth trauma or from having whooping cough during infancy were eight times more likely than other children to develop inattention, hyperactivity, and impulsivity.

Abuse, neglect, emotional and physical trauma, stress, and poor nutrition early in life also increase the risk for ADHD. Children who are deprived of good nutrition, who witness violence in the home or community, who are neglected, or who are physically, sexually, or verbally abused are at especially high risk. In fact, in 2016 neuroscientist Martin H. Teicher and psychologist Jacqueline Samson reviewed research on the effects of childhood mistreatment and concluded that being mistreated in childhood accounts for 45 percent of the risk for developing any childhood mental disorder. Their research also indicates that mistreatment or neglect during childhood disrupts brain development in ways that can lead to or worsen ADHD in genetically susceptible children. Specifically, mistreatment can disrupt the development of communications networks within the cerebral cortex and between the cortex and parts of the brain involved in regulating executive functions. These disruptions "may result in a diminished capacity to regulate impulses and emotions, accurately attribute thoughts and intentions to others, and to be mindful of oneself,"[28] write Teicher and Samson.

Brain Basics

The human brain contains about 100 billion nerve cells, or neurons. Neurons consist of a cell body that contains the genetic material and other tiny organs that run the cell, along with a long extension called an axon and several shorter extensions called dendrites. Neurons communicate with other neurons using chemical signals. The cell axon releases a chemical called a neurotransmitter into a tiny gap between neurons called a synapse. Receptors on the dendrites of other neurons take in the neurotransmitter. Groups of neurons that communicate with each other in this way are called brain circuits or networks.

Different types of neurons release and take up different neurotransmitters. Some neurotransmitters, like glutamate, are excitatory, meaning they activate and make a receiving neuron fire electrically. The electrical pulse stimulates that neuron to release a neurotransmitter to stimulate still other neurons.

Other neurotransmitters, such as gamma-amino butyric acid, are inhibitory, meaning they prevent neurons that absorb the neurotransmitter from firing. The nervous system depends on delicate balances between excitatory and inhibitory neurotransmitters to function optimally.

If an individual's brain lacks enough of a certain neurotransmitter, or if receptors fail to take in enough neurotransmitter, disorders like ADHD may result. In fact, people with ADHD lack enough of the neurotransmitters dopamine and norepinephrine. Other brain abnormalities that contribute to ADHD are underdeveloped connections between the frontal lobes of the cerebral cortex, the "thinking" part of the brain, and areas under the cortex that govern attention, learning, memory, emotional regulation, and executive function.

Studies showing that parenting practices affect the development and severity of ADHD have led some experts and many in the general public to conclude that bad parenting causes the disorder. However, the consensus among experts is that even though harsh parenting can worsen ADHD, it cannot cause ADHD unless an individual has a genetic predisposition to develop it.

Complex Interactions

What is clear is that the interactions between biological and environmental factors that cause ADHD are complex. Sometimes it is difficult to untangle which factors cause ADHD and which ones are caused by the disorder. For instance, studies by Gordon T. Harold, a psychology professor at the University of Sussex in Great Britain, analyzed the effects of hostility from adoptive mothers on children with a genetic risk for ADHD. Harold found that a mother's hostile behavior worsened symptoms of hyperactivity and impulsivity in children who were adopted at birth. However, annoying behavior in kids with ADHD also triggered hostile behavior in the mother, and this behavior further exacerbated out-of-control behavior in the child. The causes and effects of ADHD thus interact in complex ways.

Studies on parents who have ADHD also shed light on the complexity of these genetic and environmental interactions. Numerous studies find that parents with ADHD have difficulties controlling and supervising their children. According to ADHD experts Charlotte Johnston and Andrea Chronis-Tuscano, these difficulties result in "harsh or overreactive discipline, lax or inconsistent discipline, poor monitoring of child behavior, chaotic homes with poor routines and structure, and harsh responses to children's expressions of emotion."[29] Such behaviors in parents can worsen a child's ADHD symptoms, which can further exacerbate the tendency of the parent with ADHD to behave in ways that elevate the level of hostility and disorganization in the home.

Studies on the interactions between mutations in the serotonin transporter gene and environmental stressors also shed light on how these interactions contribute to causing or worsening ADHD. Several studies indicate that these mutations make children especially sensitive to all types of environmental stressors. A study published in 2016 by psychologist Alexis Elmore and her colleagues at the University of Iowa shows how a child's home environment interacts with this sensitivity to influence the

Parents with ADHD might have difficulties controlling and supervising their children. This can lead to chaotic homes with poor routines and structure, which can contribute to the existence of ADHD in their children.

severity of ADHD symptoms. Elmore's team found that children with the serotonin transporter gene mutation and ADHD who live with parents who practice harsh discipline and constantly criticize the child are far more likely to have severe inattention problems than are kids with the mutation and ADHD who live with warm, caring parents.

How Do Events Trigger ADHD?

The complex interactions between a genetic predisposition and adverse experiences can, in turn, trigger ADHD through a variety of mechanisms. One such mechanism is epigenetic changes in brain circuits that involve self-regulation. Epigenetics is the study of how experiences change the expression of genes without changing the underlying molecular structure. Gene expression

Brain Damage and ADHD

A study published in March 2018 by researchers at the Kennedy Krieger Institute in Baltimore sheds light on how brain abnormalities contribute to causing ADHD. The researchers used high-resolution magnetic resonance imaging to obtain detailed images of the brains of four- and five-year-old children with ADHD. They found that children with the most extensive brain abnormalities showed the most severe symptoms of inattention, hyperactivity, and impulsivity. The brain abnormalities in this case consisted of size reductions in the frontal, parietal, and temporal lobes of the cortex in areas that govern attention, motor activity, and decision making. Biologists divide the brain's cortex into four sections, or lobes: the frontal, parietal, occipital, and temporal lobes.

One finding that surprised the researchers and other neuroscientists was that the structural brain abnormalities underlying ADHD could be seen in four- and five-year-olds. Previous imaging studies of brain abnormalities in ADHD used school-aged children, so no one knew whether such damage was visible in younger children. According to research psychologist James A. Griffin of the Eunice Kennedy Shriver National Institute of Child Health and Human Development, "Researchers were expecting to find the beginning signs of possible atypical brain development. What they found in their high-resolution scans was solid evidence that these structural changes already are prominent by age 4 or 5."

Quoted in National Institutes of Health, "Atypical Brain Development Observed in Preschoolers with ADHD Symptoms," News Releases, March 26, 2018. www.nih.gov.

is the process in which cells translate instructions contained in genes into doing what the cell is supposed to do. When experiences produce epigenetic changes, these changes can either impair or enhance gene expression in specific genes.

In 2013 researchers at Hefei Technology University in China found that exposure to lead causes epigenetic changes that enhance the expression of mutated dopamine transport genes and dopamine receptor genes in rats. The exposure therefore makes hyperactive rats more hyperactive. According to the researchers, their study was the first to establish "an epigenetic bridge . . . linking the environmental factor [lead] and the genetic factor (disease-related genes' expression) with ADHD."[30] The mechanism by which the epigenetic changes occur is called histone acetylation. Histones are proteins in DNA—the molecules that make up genes—that influence gene expression. Exposure to lead increases the activity of these proteins and thus increases expression of the mutated genes.

Researchers find that some epigenetic changes can be stored and inherited just like genes themselves are inherited. "In effect, they 'ride along' on the DNA in inheritance," Nigg writes. "The DNA brings with it a chemical memory of some of the parents' experiences (both fathers' and mothers') and passes it to the child."[31] Several studies indicate that epigenetic changes can also be overridden or undone. For example, studies on laboratory animals indicate that giving pregnant females nutritional supplements can prevent epigenetic changes that result from a fetus's exposure to bisphenol, a toxic plastic. Other studies show that epigenetic changes that result from high levels of stress hormones circulating in human pregnant mothers can be prevented with exercise.

> "[In epigenetics,] the DNA brings with it a chemical memory of some of the parents' experiences (both fathers' and mothers') and passes it to the child."[31]
>
> —Psychologist, ADHD expert, and researcher Joel T. Nigg

Direct Damage

Epigenetic changes are only one way in which events can contribute to causing ADHD. Adverse events can also directly damage or slow development in or between brain areas that play a role in thinking, emotion, memory, and executive function. For example, in a 2016 study, Teicher and Samson found that negative early experiences like abuse or neglect lead to the production of toxic amounts of chemicals such as cortisol in the body. Cortisol is a so-called stress hormone that is necessary for regulating metabolism, immune function, blood pressure, mood, and more, but too much of it is detrimental to brain development. In fact, too much cortisol can lead to an abnormally small prefrontal cortex, hippocampus, and amygdala—all of which are important in learning, memory, and emotional control. When coupled with an inherited predisposition to ADHD, these deficiencies can trigger the disorder.

Although most studies on trauma-related brain damage focus on early childhood experiences, there is evidence that mistreatment during adolescence can also lead to lasting brain damage that can in turn raise the risk of ADHD. Neuroscientist Jay N. Giedd has studied brain development extensively and notes that the human brain undergoes the most rapid development during the first years of life and during adolescence. During these periods, the brain has what neuroscientists call heightened plasticity, or an increased ability to learn, change, and adapt. But as Giedd explains, "plasticity is a double-edged sword. It allows teenagers to make enormous strides in thinking and socialization. But the morphing landscape also makes them vulnerable to dangerous behaviors and serious mental disorders."[32] One area that undergoes the most significant changes during adolescence is the prefrontal cortex. Since this area is so vulnerable to change during these years, trauma that damages it can result in lasting impairments in decision making and emotional regulation.

Brain Arousal and ADHD

Other research shows how certain gene mutations and brain damage can cause ADHD by leading to defects in the processes that regulate the brain's state of arousal or alertness. The brain may become underaroused, which leads to inattention, or overaroused, which leads to a barrage of incoming stimuli that overwhelms an individual's ability to focus on any one thing.

A study published in 2016 by a team of researchers led by psychiatrist Michael Halassa of the Massachusetts Institute of Technology ties brain arousal and subsequent ADHD symptoms

The human brain undergoes rapid development during adolescence. This rapid change leaves teens more vulnerable to dangerous behaviors and serious mental disorders.

to a gene mutation that leads to defects in neuron communications. The team found that abnormalities in a gene called *PTCHD1* (patched-domain containing protein 1) disrupts communications between brain relay and coordination centers in the thalamus and the cerebral cortex in mice. The thalamus is located between the midbrain and the cerebral cortex. It plays a critical role in filtering and processing sensory signals before sending appropriate information to the cortex. It also coordinates behavior and movement by managing the flow of brain signals in various other parts of the brain.

Halassa's team based their experiments on previous studies showing that people with defective *PTCHD1* genes have trouble with attention and suffer from hyperactivity and sleep abnormalities. The researchers "knocked out," or deleted, the *PTCHD1* gene in mice to confirm that a defective or missing *PTCHD1* gene has the same effects in mice. These mice displayed symptoms identical to those seen in people with defective *PTCHD1* genes.

The researchers then traced brain communication networks in the mice and determined that *PTCHD1* normally regulates activity in a part of the thalamus called the thalamic reticular nucleus (TRN). The TRN filters out distracting information before transmitting sensory signals to the cortex. This allows the cortex to focus on what is important when it engages in decision making and other higher thought processes.

The TRN in mice that lack the *PTCHD1* gene cannot filter out distractions before sending signals to the cortex, so, like people with ADHD, these mice become overwhelmed with incoming neural signals that overarouse the brain. Halassa's team discovered that the underlying biochemical reason for this defect is that without a *PTCHD1* gene, neurons in the mouse TRN cannot move potassium from inside the cell across the membrane that encloses the cell. Potassium movement is needed to allow TRN neurons to create and transmit electrical signals that activate other TRN neurons that are responsible for filtering incoming sensory information. As a result, filtering does not occur. According to Halassa, this study helps explain "how the brain's processing of sensory information, a key impairment in autism and ADHD, can affect higher cognitive functions, such as attention and decision-making. Low-level disruption from an inability to focus can lead to higher level problems with memory, thinking, and long-term learning."[33]

> "Low-level disruption from an inability to focus can lead to higher level problems with memory, thinking, and long-term learning."[33]
>
> —Psychiatrist and researcher Michael Halassa

Slow Brain Processing

Another way in which brain abnormalities cause typical ADHD symptoms is by slowing down the brain's ability to process and respond to incoming information. A series of studies at the University of Gottingen in Germany illustrates how this happens. The researchers placed electrodes on the scalps of children with and without ADHD and recorded the brain waves that were generated when the children responded to a visual warning signal on a computer game. The brains of children without ADHD showed a spike of activity approximately two hundred milliseconds after the signal appeared. This indicated that the brain detected and processed the signal. But the brains of kids with ADHD showed either no activity or very little activity after the signal appeared. These children also did not respond to the signal. "This indicates that the warning was not registering in the brain even though they were looking at the screen,"[34] states Nigg in a comment about the research.

These findings help explain how and why children with ADHD have difficulty processing information and making decisions. Because their brains process and sort incoming information very slowly or not at all, they often must make a decision before they have had time to fully process the information. This might happen in a classroom, where the teacher is giving the class instructions about a homework assignment. A child with ADHD will not process the information quickly enough to determine whether the teacher said to complete math problems on page nine or page ten, and this train of thought will become lost as the child tries to move on to follow the rest of the conversation. The child will thus not know or remember what homework was assigned. Debbie, a young woman with ADHD, describes how the inability to quickly process information affects her in everyday life: "When something's important, like directions, or something that has to do with a sequence, I can't follow it. I can't hear the information and store it,"[35] she says.

Understanding the biological and molecular causes of ADHD symptoms helps scientists and therapists devise new methods of assisting people with the disorder. For example, developing new drugs that help speed up neural processing or implementing special education techniques that give students with ADHD extra time to process information are just two possible remedies that might prove to be effective.

Chapter 3

What Is It Like to Live with ADHD?

Life can be challenging for individuals with ADHD and their families. Dealing with the attention, emotion, thinking, and behavior issues involved in the disorder is often overwhelming and frustrating. Jessica McCabe, who runs a YouTube channel called How to ADHD, notes that each day is "a rollercoaster of successes and failures. . . . Adventure and (somewhat) controlled chaos are my constant companions."[36]

Even those with ADHD who receive treatment that diminishes their symptoms still deal with the consequences of poor self-regulation. Indeed, researchers find that the capacity for self-regulation influences life success more than IQ, school performance, or home environment. As Roy F. Baumeister, Brandon J. Schmeichel, and Kathleen D. Vohs explain, self-regulation is "a key to success in human life and, when it falls short, a contributing cause that helps explain many forms of human suffering."[37] Studies show that people who cannot self-regulate are more likely than others to end up failing in school, abusing drugs, and having unhealthy relationships, and they are more prone to illness. For instance, studies by researchers at the University of Pittsburgh indicate that teens and young adults with ADHD are more than twice as likely as their peers to abuse marijuana and other drugs. Overcoming these odds and forging a satisfying life with ADHD therefore takes much effort and persistence.

Diagnosis Brings Relief

The challenges associated with ADHD emerge well before a diagnosis is made. Indeed, behavior and learning difficulties are the reasons why parents of kids with ADHD seek professional help in the first place. Many people are diagnosed in early childhood, but some are not and struggle to understand why they have so many problems in school and other aspects of life. Max, for instance, had problems with inattention and hyperactivity starting in preschool. He often lay on the floor in his own world or bounced from one thing to another without understanding why. Receiving a diagnosis of severe combined-type ADHD at age eight was a relief because it helped him understand his behavior.

> "Adventure and (somewhat) controlled chaos are my constant companions."[36]
>
> —Jessica McCabe, who has ADHD and runs the YouTube channel How to ADHD

Donna Reames, who was not diagnosed with ADHD until she reached adulthood, found the diagnosis gave her hope of doing something about her problems. "All my life, I had struggled with a vague sense that something was different about me," she states. "I felt inferior, inadequate, undisciplined, and hopelessly disorganized—all feelings that have been, at one time or another, reinforced by others in my life . . . until I finally met someone who listened to my story and gave me a chance to do something about it."[38]

Feeling Overwhelmed

Receiving a diagnosis is the first step toward managing ADHD, but living with the disorder can still be overwhelming after diagnosis and treatment. Joanne Griffin, for instance, describes how

Teens with ADHD are more than twice as likely as their peers to abuse drugs. Those with ADHD typically have poor self-regulation, which can lead to self-destructive behaviors.

she felt an overwhelming need to escape from her school as a child because she could not focus or understand what was being taught: "My classes were so overwhelming. I remember staring at the classroom doorknob, wanting to run away. So I did. I just left school and walked home one day."[39]

ADHD expert and psychiatrist Edward Hallowell, who has the disorder himself, understands why he and others with ADHD tend to feel overwhelmed. He says the failure of his brain to filter incoming information leads to a constant barrage of incoming sensations and perceptions that literally overwhelm his brain with irrelevant details. The resulting jumble prevents him from paying attention, controlling his emotions, and making decisions. "It's like having a Ferrari engine for a brain, but with bicycle brakes,"[40] Hallowell explains.

Kelly Schmidt, whose son has ADHD, writes that she understands how being overwhelmed with neural input leads to what she calls "analysis paralysis"[41] in her son. This is why he and others with ADHD have trouble making seemingly simple decisions. For instance, Schmidt states, taking her child to an ice cream shop that offers a choice of thirty-one flavors would be a huge mistake because he would be overwhelmed with all the choices and become agitated. Knowing this, Schmidt realized that a similar thing would happen if her son had to choose what he wanted for lunch in the school cafeteria, even though the only choices were a hot lunch, a cheese sandwich, a turkey sandwich, or yogurt. So she decided that she would pack a lunch for him to take to school each day, thereby helping him avoid one source of overwhelming stress in his daily life.

> "It's like having a Ferrari engine for a brain, but with bicycle brakes."[40]
>
> —Psychiatrist and ADHD expert Edward Hallowell, who has ADHD

Social Difficulties

Another immense challenge for people with ADHD is that their behaviors often lead to social difficulties and a poor self-image. Numerous studies, including a 2017 study reported by researchers at Florida International University, find that children and adolescents with ADHD have high levels of rejection by peers and lower than average levels of social skills and social awareness.

When children with ADHD poke and push other kids and talk nonstop, their behavior is bound to annoy their peers. Often, other kids tend to isolate children with ADHD and may tease them. Many kids with the disorder also have difficulties with both fine and large motor skills, and this makes it difficult for them to throw a baseball, ride a bicycle, write, draw, cut paper, or tie shoelaces. As a result, classmates may avoid choosing them for sports teams or may tease them about being unintelligent.

The fact that kids with ADHD often do poorly in school and fail to complete tasks in general also feeds criticism from parents, classmates, and teachers about being unintelligent and lazy. Sarah, for example, states that as a child and beyond, she faced an endless barrage of comments from others: "You are told you're lazy, not trying hard enough, a space cadet, and that you aren't living up to your potential. [People say] you'd lose your head if it wasn't attached."[42]

Such criticism often frustrates children with ADHD and diminishes their self-esteem. Indeed, studies show that children with ADHD tend to simply feel unloved and rejected; they are often not aware that others may avoid or criticize them because these individuals find them to be obnoxious. Being constantly criticized by parents, teachers, and peers and not being invited to birthday parties makes many children with ADHD feel stupid, lazy, and unlikable.

These negative effects on self-esteem often lead kids with ADHD to lash out in anger or to display additional negative behaviors, which can lead to a vicious cycle of aggression, impulsivity, and other disruptive behaviors. In some cases, a child's frustrations about social difficulties and attempts to make friends can lead to show-off behavior. The child may do dangerous things like jumping off a staircase, climbing on a roof, or stealing from a teacher in an effort to be liked and accepted as competent. Because of these disruptive behaviors, kids with ADHD are more likely than others to be suspended from preschool, day care, elementary school, and middle or high school.

Taking Responsibility

Like other people who have social difficulties, many children, teens, and adults with ADHD say they wish others would simply accept them for who they are and not try to change their behavior. For instance, Nick, a young adult with ADHD, states that as a child he wished others would simply accept him rather than

A Lack of Self-Awareness

According to psychologist Russell Barkley, often when children and teenagers with ADHD are rude to others and monopolize conversations, they are not really aware that they are doing something wrong or that others do not want to befriend them because of these behaviors. Barkley calls this tendency "a form of ego protection." In essence, it is an unconscious attempt to protect the self from being labeled as a bad person.

Studies by psychologist Emma Sciberras and her colleagues at the Royal Children's Hospital in Australia support this assessment. They found that children with ADHD have inflated opinions of their own competence in school and social situations, compared to the opinions of their parents, teachers, and doctors. For instance, in one study 81 percent of the kids and 52 percent of their parents said the child can "get along with other kids." Sixty percent of the children and 44 percent of their parents said the child can "learn things quickly."

Along the same lines, many kids with ADHD also do not understand the aim of punishment for bad behavior. This may lead them to ignore any such consequences. One mother, for example, notes that "punishment just rolls off his back. . . . He's almost immune to anything we do." In some cases, experts say, kids with ADHD purposely ignore punishment and other attempts at behavior control to be defiant. But usually, they ignore these measures because they do not understand the purpose.

Quoted in Lesley Alderman, "Living with ADHD: Max's Story," Everyday Health. www.everydayhealth.com.

Emma Sciberras et al., "The Child's Experience of ADHD," *Journal of Attention Disorders*, vol. 15, no. 4, 2011, p. 324.

Quoted in Paul H. Wender and David A. Tomb, *ADHD*. 5th ed. New York: Oxford University Press, 2017, p. 27.

harping about how bad it was to be hyperactive and to not complete or follow through with schoolwork. Rather than telling him he needed to behave better, Nick states, he would have preferred having others ask him "what life is like . . . without trying to fix everything."[43] Others say they just wish parents, teachers, and peers would offer criticism in a calm, constructive way rather than insisting that someone whose attention wanders and who cannot sit still is somehow lazy, defiant, and a complete failure.

Participation in team sports can be a good opportunity for youth with ADHD to become more socially adept. In a team environment they learn to respect, work with, and support their peers.

However, although most experts agree that being calm and constructive is a good thing, they also believe that allowing a child to excuse or blame his behavior on ADHD is not a good idea. Even though ADHD has a biological basis, explain psychiatrists Paul H. Wender and David A. Tomb, people with the disorder are capable of controlling and improving their behavior. "The ADHD child does better when he is held accountable and made responsible for his behavior," they write. "He should not be allowed to say, either in so many words or indirectly, 'I'm ADHD—I'm a mental cripple—I'm not responsible for what I do."[44] Wender and Tomb note that kids who take responsibility for their behavior are more likely to overcome their difficulties with learning and social interaction and to live productive lives as adults with ADHD.

A child can learn about the value of this type of responsibility from a therapist or parent who uses role-playing exercises or other methods of practicing proper behavior to help him or her become more socially adept and cognizant of right and wrong. Other times the realization stems from activities like team sports, as the mother of a nine-year-old named Matthew explains in an *ADDitude* magazine article. For years, this mother desperately wished that Matthew had friends. However, she explains, "He pushed away every kid who tried to be his friend. His play was so chaotic that others had a hard time wanting to be around him." Finally, Matthew started participating in team sports. His mother observes that "he started to realize everything wasn't about him. . . . After two seasons of baseball and two seasons of football, we are now seeing him develop healthy friendships."[45]

ADHD in Adolescence

Some kids with ADHD continue to have extreme social difficulties throughout their childhood or even throughout their lives. However, many begin to understand social rules and start to get along better with others when they reach adolescence. Often, symptoms of hyperactivity also diminish in adolescence, and this helps with both social and academic challenges. But this is not always true, and experts find that many times, difficulties in teens with ADHD stem from not being ready to self-manage. As clinical psychologist Mary Rooney explains, "Developmentally, teenagers are expected to be able to handle more autonomy: less structure in their school and home lives and less teacher and parental oversight."[46] But since brain development in teens with ADHD lags behind that of other teens, many find new opportunities for independence to be confusing.

Some of these teens find themselves overwhelmed by having to go to multiple classrooms and having to handle homework in multiple subjects in middle and high school. Some kids with ADHD are so far behind in school by the time they reach adolescence that they never catch up. For example, Carolyn Mallon found that her academic difficulties increased in high school because of her lack of focus and organizational skills: "I would try to follow the class lecture, but if I lost track of what they were discussing, I might as well have wandered alone in the woods. I just couldn't catch up. After a while, I started skipping classes to avoid the shame and embarrassment of having no assignment to turn in or knowing I was going to flunk a test."[47]

Frustration about academic and social demands in high school contributes to the fact that teens with ADHD are more likely to fail classes and to drop out of school. One large-scale study by researchers at several US universities found that high school students with ADHD failed 7.5 percent of their courses, compared to students without ADHD failing 1.7 percent. The CDC also notes that students with ADHD are more than three times more likely to drop out of school than their peers.

But for many with ADHD, adolescence is a time when they settle down enough to accept help from teachers, parents, and tutors and improve their school performance. Learning specific ways of compensating for ADHD—for instance, learning to write down all assignments and daily tasks in a notebook, doing homework in a quiet place with no distractions, and breaking down large tasks into smaller ones—can improve overall functioning and influence school success. Individualized IEPs in school can also help. For example, having a teenager with ADHD sit near the teacher, arranging for the teacher to give the child extra time to complete a test or homework, or allowing a classmate to take notes in class for the teen with ADHD are all accommodations that can improve success in school.

For many with ADHD, adolescence is a time when they settle down enough to accept help from teachers and parents to improve their school performance. They develop skills that compensate for the challenges of ADHD.

Driving Is a Challenge

Another area in which teens with ADHD face challenges is driving a car. A college student with ADHD named Michael, for example, was cited for more than ten moving violations, including speeding, running red lights, and driving drunk, by age twenty. His license was revoked for a year after he was caught driving drunk. According to studies by psychologists Russell Barkley and Daniel J. Cox, inattention, distractibility, and impulsivity make teens with ADHD far more likely than their peers to speed and disobey other traffic laws when driving, to drive without a license, and to have their driver's license revoked. Teenagers with ADHD are also two to four times more likely to cause traffic accidents.

Taking ADHD medication does help these teens improve their driving skills. A 2017 study at the Karolinska Institutet in Sweden found that young men with ADHD had a 38 percent lower risk of crashing when taking ADHD medication, and young women had a 42 percent lower risk, compared with unmedicated people with ADHD. However, psychologist Marlene Snyder notes that even those who are being treated may not be mature enough to drive. "Young people with ADHD are often emotionally and functionally immature when compared to their peers," Snyder writes. "Teenagers with ADHD may take significantly longer to develop good judgement and a mature attitude toward driving."[48] For this reason, Barkley and Cox recommend that teens and their parents develop and sign a driving contract that specifies what rules must be followed—for instance, no cell phones, no food, no alcohol, and so on—and that spells out the consequences for non-compliance to ensure that teens are mature enough to understand their responsibilities before they start driving.

> "Young people with ADHD are often emotionally and functionally immature when compared to their peers. Teenagers with ADHD may take significantly longer to develop good judgement and a mature attitude toward driving."[48]
>
> —Psychologist Marlene Snyder

ADHD Affects Families

Living with ADHD is not only challenging for the individual with the disorder but also for his or her family. Parents may experience stress and frustration because of the behaviors of a child or teen with ADHD. They may become angry because of the child's disobedience, inattention, and disorganized behavior. They may nag, criticize, or harshly punish the child or may emotionally disengage from the child, which leads to guilt, frustration, diminished self-esteem, and even severe depression and anxiety for all involved. According to researchers at Maastricht University and Utrecht University in the Netherlands,

> Parents of children with Attention Deficit Hyperactivity Disorder (ADHD) are less rewarding and consistent, display lower levels of warmth and involvement, and more often use physical discipline in comparison to parents of children without ADHD. When children become more negative in their behavior, they are harder to discipline, which leads to parents using even more aversive strategies. In this way, families become entangled in a downward spiral of negativity.[49]

Improving Driver Safety in Teens with ADHD

Studies show that teens with ADHD are far less likely than other teens to drive safely. Clinical psychologist Jeffrey N. Epstein and his colleagues at the Cincinnati Children's Hospital Medical Center are therefore conducting research on methods of improving driver safety among these teens. "Teens with Attention-Deficit Hyperactivity Disorder (ADHD) have high rates of negative driving outcomes, including motor vehicle crashes, which may be caused by visual inattention (i.e., looking away from the roadway to perform secondary tasks)," explain the researchers. In fact, other studies find that teen drivers with ADHD glance away from the roadway three times more often than other teen drivers. This significantly increases their risk of causing an accident. Overall, a 2017 study by researchers at Children's Hospital of Pennsylvania found that teens with ADHD have a 36 percent higher risk of crashing while driving than their peers.

Epstein's team is assessing the effectiveness of what they call "a driving intervention that trains teens [with ADHD] to reduce instances of looking away from the roadway." The intervention, known as Focused Concentration and Attention Learning (FOCAL+), is a computer-based program that educates teens about the dangers of extended glances away from the road and trains them to limit the length of such glances. A camera placed in the cars of participating teens is recording each teen's driving behavior before and after he or she undergoes the training. The researchers are also tracking each teen's driving record to assess whether the program is effective.

ClinicalTrials.gov, "Improving ADHD Teen Driving," US National Library of Medicine. https://clinicaltrials.gov.

Psychiatrist Linda J. Pfiffner and psychologist Lauren Haack call this vicious cycle of negative behaviors the "coercive process"[50] because parents and children are controlling each other's behavior through their own responses. For example, when a child with ADHD ignores a parent's request to do his homework, the parent may respond by yelling or perhaps spanking him, which angers the child and makes him even more defiant, which escalates the parent's anger, and so on.

Cristina Margolis, who has a seven-year-old daughter with ADHD, writes that she feels guilty about losing patience with the girl but finds it difficult to cope with her ongoing defiance:

> When I see her little sister, three years younger than my daughter, listen to me and behave the way I expect her to, I praise her and reward her. When her older sister can't do the same simple things—sit down at the table for dinner or get into her pajamas without complaining—I get frustrated. I lose patience. I blow up, particularly at the end of the day, when I am physically and emotionally drained.[51]

Stress also leads to interpersonal conflicts within the family. Parents often bicker over the proper way to discipline and deal with the child with ADHD. Parents also spend extra time securing proper care and services from schools and doctors for their child with ADHD. In addition, the child needs extra attention to help finish homework and chores. This often makes siblings feel left out. One sibling comments that "everything revolved around my brother and it almost was like it had to go his way."[52] Another says, "My needs would always be ignored."[53] Siblings also report being embarrassed by the behavior of the child with ADHD and hesitating to invite friends to their home as a consequence. Many also state that they resent being forced to supervise and take responsibility for ensuring the safety of a sibling with ADHD.

Overall, studies that ask siblings of children with ADHD about the impact on their families find that the effects are serious and ongoing. One study reports that siblings "become tired and exasperated living with their brother or sister with ADHD, swinging between love, resentment and envy."[54] Another study notes that siblings speak of "resentment, embarrassment and guilt," and in still another study, siblings describe family life as "chaotic, conflictual and exhausting . . . [filled with] never-ending . . . daily disruption."[55] Many siblings also report being hit or threatened by the child with ADHD and thus becoming fearful of their sibling. Many people find that joining support groups consisting of families going through the same problems can help the entire family develop strategies for coping with the many challenges they face.

The Positives

Although living with ADHD is challenging for individuals and families, many people learn to look at and harness the benefits of the positives of ADHD. As experts point out, even though people with ADHD can be hyperactive, their boundless energy can be a plus if it is channeled productively. And even though they tend to act impulsively and may not plan ahead, they are often good at improvising in difficult situations. As a report by economist Johan Wiklund and his colleagues puts it, being impulsive "facilitates decision making in complex and uncertain situations."[56]

Many people with ADHD are also extremely creative and turn new ideas into novel inventions and/or thriving businesses because they are less averse to taking risks than others. A business owner named Cathy, for example, states that her ADHD motivates her to be open to trying new things and to feel "at ease and stimulated in situations that may cause anxiety for others, such as engaging with new prestigious customers."[57] And a business owner named George says his impulsivity enhances his productivity; he would not accomplish as much as he does each day if he carefully analyzed each decision before taking action.

The tendency for people with ADHD to hyperfocus on things that truly interest them can also have positive results, especially once they mature and learn to channel their energies productively. For example, a man with ADHD named Pete became fascinated with producing television shows as a child. He learned everything he could about the subject and launched a successful production business as a young man. He became a noted expert in his field.

In a similar manner, even though people with ADHD tend to talk too much, many are very sociable and fun to be with if they learn to rein in their tendency to interrupt others. An article about a teenager named Max, for example, points out that his immaturity and constant banter endeared him to younger children when he served as a camp counselor while he was in high school. In fact, despite the challenges of living with ADHD, many individuals and families say they appreciate the many special qualities that make people with ADHD outstanding human beings. As a mom named Lisa states, "My son has empathy borne of his own ongoing struggle. He can find the good in any person, recognizing that 'Each person comes with their own strengths and challenges—that's just human, Mom!'"[58]

Chapter 4

Can ADHD Be Treated or Cured?

There is no cure for ADHD, but available drug and behavior treatments help many with the disorder lead satisfying and productive lives. The goal of treatment is to reduce symptoms and improve people's general quality of life. In line with this goal, the National Institute of Neurological Disorders and Stroke (NINDS) explains that whereas ADHD medications primarily address specific symptoms, various types of therapy help children with ADHD function better in school, at home, and in other situations. "Most experts agree that treatment for ADHD should address multiple aspects of the individual's functioning and should not be limited to the use of medications alone," states the NINDS website. "Treatment should include structured classroom management, parent education (to address discipline and limit-setting), and tutoring and/or behavioral therapy for the child."[59] Indeed, a long-term study known as the Multimodal Treatment Study indicates that a combination of drugs and psychosocial/behavior therapy gives the best results.

According to the CDC, in 2016, 62 percent of the children diagnosed with ADHD in the United States—about 3.3 million children—were taking medication. At the same time, 46.7

percent—about 2.5 million children—were receiving behavior therapy. Another 31.7 percent were receiving both medication and behavior therapy, and 23 percent received no treatment.

Studies indicate that a lack of treatment increases the risk for numerous undesirable consequences. For this reason, public health agencies and ADHD experts emphasize the importance of receiving a diagnosis and following a physician's recommendations for a treatment plan that is tailored to meet individual needs.

According to CHADD, children with ADHD who receive no treatment are likely to experience increasing difficulties in school and to develop severe behavior problems that can lead to criminal and antisocial behavior. Untreated children are also more likely to injure themselves and to require care in hospital emergency rooms because of wild and impulsive behavior. Overall, states an article by researchers at the University of Iowa, "untreated ADHD can pose a tremendous amount of psychological, financial, academic, and social burden to the individual and the community."[60] Early treatment decreases, but does not erase, these higher risks.

> "Untreated ADHD can pose a tremendous amount of psychological, financial, academic, and social burden to the individual and the community."[60]
>
> —A 2015 study by Alaa M. Hamed and colleagues at the University of Iowa

Drug Treatment

The main drugs used to treat ADHD are stimulant drugs like methylphenidate (brand names Ritalin, Concerta, and Focalin) and amphetamines (brand names Adderall and Vyvanse). It may seem counterintuitive that stimulants calm down hyperactive children. Indeed, when psychiatrist Charles Bradley discovered that the stimulant Benzedrine calmed hyperactive kids during the 1930s, he, too, was baffled. Bradley originally gave Benzedrine to kids with neurological diseases who developed headaches. He discovered that the drug did not alleviate the headaches, but it did calm children who were prone to emotional outbursts and hyperactivity. In a 1937 report he wrote for the *American Journal of Psychiatry*, Bradley stated, "There was a spectacular improvement in school performance in half of the children. A large proportion of the patients became emotionally subdued without, however, losing interest in their surroundings."[61] Bradley also noted that Benzedrine was usually used to provide emotional and mental stimulation for adults with severe depression, but it seemed to have the opposite effect in hyperactive children.

For many years, experts did not understand why stimulants had this apparent paradoxical effect in children. But these effects made more sense when physicians realized that ADHD is about a lack of control over executive function rather than simply being about hyperactivity. Studies proved that low doses of stimulants increase the amount of dopamine in the brain's prefrontal cortex, and this enhances control over attention, behavior, and more. Some stimulants also increase the amount of the neurotransmitter

To avoid distraction, a high school student with ADHD takes a test in an office at her school. Many schools provide classroom structure accommodations to help students with ADHD.

norepinephrine, which plays a role in alertness. Other studies, particularly those by David Erlij, a professor of physiology and pharmacology at the State University of New York Downstate Medical Center in Brooklyn, proved that stimulant drugs inhibit motor activity and thus diminish hyperactivity by stimulating dopamine receptors called D4 receptors in the basal ganglia (groupings of brain cells at the base of the cortex) of the brain.

Doctors can prescribe stimulants in the form of a liquid, capsule, tablet, or skin patch, depending on individual patient needs. These drugs benefit 80 to 90 percent of the children who use them. The American Academy of Pediatrics (AAP) explains, "As glasses help

This Video Game Requires a Prescription

Doctors note that although ADHD medications can control symptoms of ADHD, they do not improve overall executive skills or cognitive functions. Behavior therapy can help with the latter; however, many families cannot take their children for regular therapy because of time or financial constraints. Researchers are therefore testing readily accessible tools that can be brought into the home. According to a research report by Duke University psychologist Scott H. Kollins and his colleagues, "Given the high demands on parents' time and resources, it is critical that available treatments for ADHD can be reasonably incorporated into a daily routine, utilized consistently by children with ADHD, and most critically implemented without the need for physician, therapist, or psychologist oversight."

In January 2018 the Duke University researchers announced that a computerized video game called EVO meets these requirements. EVO is designed to selectively activate certain brain networks that govern executive function. The Duke team found that EVO improves focus, memory, and behavior control and diminishes impulsivity in kids with ADHD when used five days per week for thirty to forty-five minutes per day.

Akili Labs, which manufactures EVO, describes it as "a first-of-its-kind prescription digital medicine." Since people will need a physician's prescription to purchase EVO, the game must be approved by the US Food and Drug Administration before it can be marketed as an ADHD treatment.

Naomi O. Davis, Jeffrey Bower, and Scott H. Kollins, "Proof-of-Concept Study of an At-Home, Engaging, Digital Intervention for Pediatric ADHD," *PlosOne*, January 11, 2018. https://journals.plos.org.

Quoted in Kenneth Bender, "Proof-of-Concept Video Game Intervention Improves Spatial Working Memory in Children with ADHD," *MD Magazine*, February 12, 2018. www.mdmag.com.

people focus their eyes to see, these medications help children with ADHD focus their thoughts better and ignore distractions."[62]

Stimulants can have side effects, including weight loss, diminished appetite, sleep problems, elevated heart rate and blood pressure, and others, but these adverse effects usually diminish after a doctor adjusts the dosage. Some parents worry about long-term use, especially when the medication diminishes a child's appetite and he or she does not grow optimally. In such cases, some parents elect to give the child what are known as medication holidays to help normalize appetite and growth. This may include not taking medication on weekends or when school is not in session. Symptoms of ADHD worsen significantly on days when the medication is not used, but in some cases the benefits of a drug holiday outweigh the risks. As clinical psychologist Thomas E. Brown notes, "For some children, it may be a good idea to a break from their usual medication for ADHD over the summer. For other kids, taking a 'drug holiday' can be a real mistake."[63] Brown suggests that a medication holiday can be a good thing for a child who is small and underweight but is not recommended for children who are extremely disruptive at home or who become aggressive or engage in risky behaviors when not taking their medications.

Other parents worry that some children and teenagers will become addicted to ADHD medications. But most studies show that when used as directed, these drugs are not addictive or dangerous. Studies also show the drugs help children's brains develop more normally and help symptoms of ADHD diminish over the long term. Overall, according to the AAP, "For most children, stimulant medications are a safe and effective way to relieve ADHD symptoms."[64]

> "For most children, stimulant medications are a safe and effective way to relieve ADHD symptoms."[64]
>
> —The American Academy of Pediatrics

Still, some kids with ADHD do not obtain positive results from stimulants or cannot tolerate them because of side effects. In such cases, nonstimulant drugs like atomoxetine (brand name Strattera) and guanfacine (brand name Intuniv) can be used to treat ADHD. These drugs mainly target norepinephrine in the brain and have a calming effect similar to that of stimulants.

Behavior Therapy

Although drug treatment is considered to be the first-line treatment for kids and teens with ADHD, researchers find that combining behavior therapy with medication produces more positive results than either type of treatment alone. Two types of behavior therapy—cognitive-behavior therapy and skills-training therapy— are known to help kids with ADHD control their behavior and improve their performance in school.

Cognitive-behavior therapy helps patients change negative thought patterns, and these changes in turn help them change their behavior. When used with young children, the therapist teaches parents to continue techniques used at therapy sessions at home. Teens with ADHD can meet with a therapist independently or with parents present.

Typically, a therapist guides a teen in identifying the problem behaviors that need to change and in understanding the difficulties he or she will encounter. Then, the therapist helps the individual develop strategies for breaking down solutions for problem behaviors into manageable steps. The teen is encouraged to practice these steps at home between therapy sessions. The teen also learns how to monitor his or her progress by clearly identifying goals for each phase. For example, if the teen wants to implement strategies for overcoming procrastination on homework, the therapist might guide him or her in thinking about procrastination as a behavior that can be changed, rather than as an insurmountable problem. Then, the therapist and client might brainstorm methods of breaking down the problem into manageable steps and setting goals for following each step.

This type of therapy helped a tenth-grader named Jane, who wanted to learn how to keep track of her homework assignments from each class so she would remember to complete them. The therapist suggested that she choose to either use a physical notebook or a computerized calendar program to start. She chose to use a notebook, and after realizing that organizing her assignments was something she could do, she came up with the idea of using colored markers to implement a color-coded assignment log for each school subject. Once she started making daily entries using this system, she took pride in continuing to brainstorm other methods of staying on track.

Skills-training therapy is similar to cognitive-behavior therapy; in fact, it is sometimes referred to as a type of cognitive-behavior therapy. The main difference is that therapists have developed specific skills-training programs to address certain skills, such as organizing schoolwork or interacting with peers. One program is the Therapist-Guided Organizational Skills Training. It was

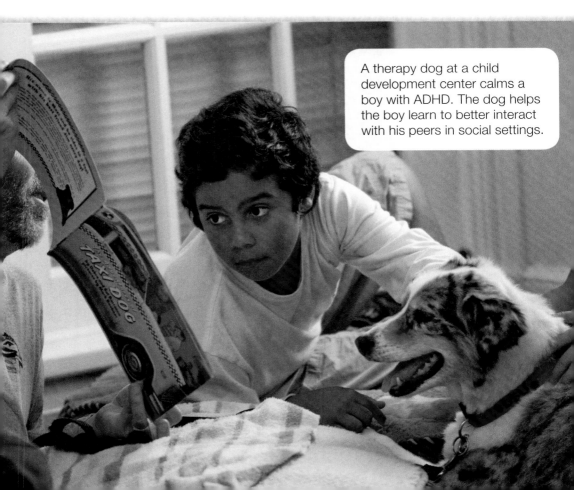

A therapy dog at a child development center calms a boy with ADHD. The dog helps the boy learn to better interact with his peers in social settings.

developed by three psychologists at New York University and based on research that shows that "many children with ADHD experience difficulties in four broad domains of organizational behavior: tracking assignments, managing materials, time management, and task planning."[65] The program guides therapists in teaching kids specific skills that address these problems. Studies show that it helps kids with ADHD dramatically improve their organizational skills at home and at school and consequently improve their grades. It is proved to also reduce parent-child conflicts at home. These effects are long lasting. The New York University psychologists report that when researchers follow up with children seven to twelve months after the training ends, they find the kids are still using the skills they were taught. These results are far better than those from therapy programs that attempt to improve overall functioning rather than teaching specific skills.

Therapists find that programs that teach kids with ADHD specific methods of improving their social skills are also very effective. For example, instructing the child to count to ten and take a deep breath before yelling at a sibling or classmate for teasing is far more effective than simply telling the child to ignore a bully.

Parent Training

Studies indicate that programs known as parent management training are also effective in improving behavior in children with ADHD. These programs train parents to not let a child's annoying behavior lead to anger and/or harsh methods of discipline. Instead, parents learn to interact calmly and use positive reinforcement with their children. Experts note that these skills are especially important in households where a child with ADHD constantly causes disruptions and stress. "Being the parent of a child with ADHD can be tiring and trying. It can test the limits of even the best parents. Parent training . . . can be a great source of help,"[66] states the AAP.

One such program is called the Behavioral Parent Training Method. It includes eight to twelve individual or group sessions,

New Data About ADHD Myths

During the late twentieth century, some parents claimed that removing food additives from their child's diet diminished ADHD symptoms. Some people also claimed that food additives cause ADHD, but scientific studies refuted such claims. However, around 2011, new studies showed that omega-3 (fish oil) supplements reduce ADHD symptoms in some children and that eliminating food additives diminishes symptoms in others who are extrasensitive to these additives.

As ADHD expert Joel T. Nigg explains, "While many other scientists and I were long skeptical of the role of food in ADHD, new and better studies just in the period from 2011 to 2015 have changed the landscape." Although studies have not proved that certain food additives cause ADHD, the new data has led Nigg and others to conclude that diet is one factor that may increase the risk of ADHD in genetically susceptible individuals. Research that builds on these findings may therefore prove that special diets can be useful in treating some people with ADHD.

However, the American Academy of Pediatrics notes that some claims, like those that blame high-sugar diets for ADHD, have proved to be myths. "There is no scientific basis for claims that sugar and other sweeteners influence behavior or cause ADHD, even at levels many times higher than in a normal diet," states the academy. "The overactivity children show after a birthday party or Halloween may be due more to the stimulation of the event than the sugar. . . . [The academy] does not recommend special diets for treating hyperactivity."

Joel T. Nigg, *Getting Ahead of ADHD.* New York: Guilford, 2017, p. 59.

American Academy of Pediatrics, "Allergies and Hyperactivity," November 21, 2015. www.healthychildren.org.

conducted either in person or online, in which therapists begin by educating parents about how positive parenting practices help build self-esteem and desirable behaviors in kids with ADHD. Therapists then teach parents how to focus on and praise the child's successes while calmly imposing time-outs or other consequences as needed to discourage the child's negative behaviors. Parents then practice these techniques at home and keep track of improvements or setbacks.

Numerous studies have found this and similar parent training programs to be effective. For example, a study published in 2015 by researchers at the Cincinnati Children's Hospital found that an eight-session Behavioral Parent Training Method program produced overwhelmingly positive effects. "The biggest effects of our program were seen in terms of improved parent-child interactions, reduced negative impact on the family, reduced overall impairments in functioning [in the child with ADHD], and improvement in parents' self-report of their confidence in managing their child's behavior,"[67] the researchers write.

Other Treatment Measures

Although drug and behavior interventions are the main elements of ADHD treatment, many experts also recommend lifestyle adjustments that can diminish ADHD symptoms and improve overall functioning. For instance, recent studies indicate that omega-3 fish oil supplements decrease ADHD symptoms in some people, so some doctors recommend that parents give these supplements to their children with ADHD. Doctors also recommend that kids with ADHD avoid ingesting anything with caffeine, as it can worsen symptoms. And, since pesticides and similar chemicals are neurotoxins, doctors advise parents to feed children with or at risk for ADHD organic foods that are not sprayed with pesticides.

In addition, physicians note that even though some parents believe food additives like artificial color may cause ADHD, researchers find no such effects. Doctors therefore advise patients that special diets are not needed. Instead, states family medicine physician David C. Agerter at the Mayo Clinic, "The best approach for overall health and nutrition is a diet that limits sugary and processed foods and is rich in fruits, vegetables, grains, and healthy fats such as omega-3 fatty acids."[68] This type of diet is recommended for overall health, regardless of whether an individual has ADHD or another disorder.

There is also evidence that regular exercise promotes growth in parts of the brain that are affected by ADHD, reduces stress,

A teenage girl drinks a caffeinated soda at a restaurant. Doctors recommend that people with ADHD avoid caffeine, as it can worsen their symptoms.

and helps diminish some symptoms of ADHD. Doctors thus advise kids with ADHD to exercise regularly, either by participating in team or individual sports or with informal activities like riding a bicycle or playing outdoors.

Getting plenty of sleep is also an important component of a treatment regimen for ADHD. Everyone needs sleep to manage stress and to allow things learned during the day to be transferred to long-term memory. But sleep is especially important for kids with ADHD because a lack of sleep worsens ADHD symptoms. In fact, many times kids who do not have ADHD exhibit ADHD-like symptoms if they do not get enough sleep.

According to CHADD, children with ADHD are two to three times likelier than other kids to have sleep-related problems. For many, hyperactivity prevents them from settling down enough to get adequate sleep. Some have trouble sleeping because of the stimulant medications used to treat ADHD. However, most of the time, taking the medication earlier in the day minimizes such effects.

Doctors recommend ten hours of sleep per night for all school-age children and nine to ten hours for teens. Sometimes simple remedies help people with ADHD get the sleep they need; avoiding blue light from electronic screens and not eating large meals or exercising for at least an hour before bedtime are often effective. If further help is needed, psychologists offer sleep-training therapies that improve sleep habits and enhance overall functioning. One 2015 study by researchers in Australia found that a behavioral sleep program significantly improved sleep, behavior, and quality of life for kids with ADHD.

Research into Improving Treatment

Although existing treatment methods can and do diminish ADHD symptoms, kids and teens with the disorder still grapple with the effects of deficits in executive function. Much research is therefore being conducted to improve existing treatments and to find new ways of helping people with ADHD.

Some researchers are creating and testing new ADHD drugs. For instance, psychiatrist Josephine Elia and her colleagues are testing an experimental drug called fasoracetam. It targets the effects of gene mutations that regulate the uptake of the neurotransmitter glutamate, which plays a role in learning, memory, and emotion. Receptors known as mGluR receptors on some nerve cell dendrites absorb glutamate released by other neurons. But as Elia's team previously discovered, 11 percent of children with ADHD have gene mutations that affect mGluR function. On the basis of this knowledge, the researchers reasoned that fasoracetam, which activates mGluR receptors, might be useful for treating ADHD in children with these mutations. Preliminary studies on teens with moderate to severe ADHD found that the drug led to so much improvement that psychiatrists downgraded their diagnoses to mild to moderate ADHD. Further tests are under way to demonstrate whether fasoracetam is truly safe and effective.

Another drug-related project seeks to address the impulsive aggressiveness displayed by some kids with ADHD. Stimulant drugs used to treat ADHD do not affect this behavior, nor are there any medications available for this purpose. Researchers at the Supernus pharmaceutical company are testing the safety and effectiveness of a drug called SPN-810, or molindone hydrochloride, in children with ADHD-related impulsive aggressiveness. It is not a new drug; it has been used in higher doses to treat schizophrenia and is known to exert calming effects by blocking some types of dopamine receptors in the brain. Often, drugs approved to treat certain diseases end up being effective for other problems. However, the Food and Drug Administration requires the manufacturer to prove the drug's safety and effectiveness for a new purpose before allowing it to be marketed for that reason.

Other studies are testing new types of behavior therapies for ADHD. Researchers at the University of Maryland, for example, are studying whether a new program called Behavioral Activation for Attention and Alcohol Disorders (BAAAD) helps college students with ADHD lead healthier lifestyles. The researchers explain that such a program is needed because other programs designed to teach students to make wiser choices on campus are notoriously ineffective in students with the high levels of impulsivity that characterize ADHD. In particular, the researchers hope the program will help students with ADHD avoid the excessive alcohol consumption that is prevalent among them. Indeed, studies indicate that 47 percent of college students with ADHD meet standards for alcohol abuse and 23 percent meet standards for alcohol dependence, compared to 12 percent and 6 percent of the general population of college students. The researchers note that the BAAAD program "teaches individuals to engage in healthy, goal-directed rewarding behaviors (e.g. academic, recreational or social activities), rather than relying on drinking to provide immediate rewards. . . . [It] has clear relevance for addressing ADHD-related executive functioning deficits."[69]

Other researchers are studying whether a nonmedical treatment that involves stimulating the trigeminal nerve is effective. Many parents say they would prefer nondrug treatments for their children, and an easy-to-use device that stimulates the trigeminal nerve may prove to give them an effective alternative. The trigeminal nerve relays sensory information from the face and head to the brain and controls the muscles involved in chewing. As researchers at the University of California, Los Angeles, explain, the nerve can be stimulated with "low current electrical stimulation via an electrode applied to the forehead and worn during sleep"[70] to activate areas of the brain that govern attention and executive function. Studies at the university thus far indicate that children with ADHD who wear the device at night for eight weeks have a 44 percent decrease in symptoms and no significant adverse side effects. In fact, trigeminal nerve stimulation has been approved as an ADHD treatment in the European Union, and the researchers hope further tests confirm that it can be approved as a safe and effective alternative in the United States.

Even with advances in understanding the causes, treatments, effects, and personal challenges posed by ADHD, experts agree there is still much work to do before the disorder can be treated effectively in all cases or, ideally, can be prevented from occurring at all. According to the CDC, "There are so many unanswered questions about ADHD,"[71] and this drives the plethora of research being conducted worldwide to gain control over this complex disorder that affects so many people of all ages.

Source Notes

Introduction: The Most Commonly Diagnosed Disorder in Kids

1. US Food and Drug Administration, "Dealing with ADHD: What You Need to Know," October 12, 2016. www.fda.gov.
2. Quoted in Caroline Miller, "Are Schools Driving ADHD Diagnoses?," Child Mind Institute. https://childmind.org.
3. Alan Schwarz, *ADHD Nation.* New York: Scribner, 2016, p. 2.
4. Quoted in Schwarz, *ADHD Nation*, p. 63.
5. Quoted in Katherine Ellison, "We Can't Afford to Treat Our ADHD," *ADDitude*, April 27, 2017. www.additudemag.com.

Chapter 1: What Is ADHD?

6. Joel T. Nigg, *Getting Ahead of ADHD*. New York: Guilford, 2017, p. 2.
7. Nigg, *Getting Ahead of ADHD*, pp. 11–12.
8. Roy F. Baumeister, Brandon J. Schmeichel, and Kathleen D. Vohs, "Self-Regulation and the Executive Function: The Self as Controlling Agent," in *Social Psychology: Handbook of Basic Principles*, edited by Arie W. Kruglanski and E. Tory Higgins. 2nd ed. New York: Guilford, 2007, p. 517.
9. Quoted in Children and Adults with Attention-Deficit/Hyperactivity Disorder, "The Science of ADHD." www.chadd.org.
10. Alexander Crichton, "On Attention, and Its Diseases," in *An Inquiry into the Nature and Origin of Mental Derangement*. Vol. 1. London: Printed for T. Cadell Jr. and W. Davies, 1798, pp. 271, 272. https://books.google.com.
11. Quoted in Klaus W. Lange et al., "The History of Attention Deficit Hyperactivity Disorder," *Attention Deficit and*

Hyperactivity Disorders, December 2010. www.ncbi.nlm.nih .gov.

12. George Frederic Still, "The Goulstonian Lectures on Some Abnormal Psychical Conditions in Children," *Lancet*, April 19, 1902.

13. Quoted in Lange et al., "The History of Attention Deficit Hyperactivity Disorder."

14. Lange et al., "The History of Attention Deficit Hyperactivity Disorder."

15. Sam D. Clements, "Minimal Brain Dysfunction in Children: Terminology and Identification Phase One of a Three-Phase Project," US Department of Health, Education, and Welfare, 1966. https://files.eric.ed.gov.

16. Understood, "Understanding ADHD." www.understood.org.

17. Children and Adults with Attention-Deficit/Hyperactivity Disorder, "Preschoolers and ADHD." www.chadd.org.

18. Quoted in John Hoffman, "What Does ADHD Really Feel Like?," *Today's Parent*, September 10, 2013. www.today sparent.com.

19. Quoted in Centers for Disease Control and Prevention, "Attention-Deficit/Hyperactivity Disorder." www.cdc.gov.

20. Quoted in Centers for Disease Control and Prevention, "Attention-Deficit/Hyperactivity Disorder."

21. Quoted in Centers for Disease Control and Prevention, "Attention-Deficit/Hyperactivity Disorder."

22. Quoted in *NIH News in Health*, "Focusing on ADHD," National Institutes of Health, September 2014. https://newsinhealth .nih.gov.

23. American Academy of Pediatrics, "Girls and ADHD," November 21, 2016. www.healthychildren.org.

24. Paul H. Wender and David A. Tomb, *ADHD*. 5th ed. New York: Oxford University Press, 2017, p. 9.

Chapter 2: What Causes ADHD?

25. Nigg, *Getting Ahead of ADHD*, p. 44.

26. Quoted in Sarah Vanbuskirk, "When ADHD Is All in the Family," *ADDitude*. www.additudemag.com.

27. Thomas E. Brown, *Attention Deficit Disorder: The Unfocused Mind in Children and Adults.* New Haven, CT: Yale University Press, 2005, p. 62.
28. Martin H. Teicher and Jacqueline Samson, "Annual Research Review: Enduring Neurobiological Effects of Childhood Abuse and Neglect," *Journal of Child Psychology and Psychiatry*, February 1, 2016, p. 255.
29. Charlotte Johnston and Andrea Chronis-Tuscano, "Families and ADHD," in *Attention-Deficit Hyperactivity Disorder*, ed. Russell Barkley. 4th ed. New York: Guilford, 2015, p. 197.
30. Man Luo et al., "Epigenetic Histone Modification Regulates Developmental Lead Exposure Induced by Hyperactivity in Rats," *Toxicology Letters*, November 2013. http://or.nsfc.gov.cn.
31. Nigg, *Getting Ahead of ADHD*, p. 51.
32. Jay N. Giedd, "The Amazing Teen Brain," *Scientific American*, June 2015, p. 34.
33. Quoted in National Institute of Mental Health, "Distractible Mice Offer Clues to Attention Deficit," Science Update March 24, 2016. www.nimh.nih.gov.
34. Nigg, *Getting Ahead of ADHD*, p. 21.
35. Quoted in *ADDitude* Editors, "What It Feels Like Living with Undiagnosed ADHD," *ADDitude*. www.additudemag.com.

Chapter 3: What Is It Like to Live with ADHD?

36. Jessica McCabe, "What the Ups and Downs of ADHD in a Day Can Look Like," Healthline, July 27, 2017. www.health line.com.
37. Baumeister, Schmeichel, and Vohs, "Self-Regulation and the Executive Function," p. 516.
38. Quoted in ADDitude Editors, "What It Feels Like Living with Undiagnosed ADHD."
39. Quoted in ADDitude Editors, "What It Feels Like Living with Undiagnosed ADHD."
40. Quoted in Denise Foley, "ADHD & Kids: The Truth about Attention Deficit Hyperactivity Disorder," Time.com. http://time .com.
41. Kelly Schmidt, "4 Things My Kid with ADHD Sees Differently," Healthline, March 29, 2017. www.healthline.com.
42. Quoted in ADDitude Editors, "What It Feels Like Living with Undiagnosed ADHD."

43. Quoted in Hoffman, "What Does ADHD Really Feel Like?"
44. Wender and Tomb, *ADHD*, pp. 95–96.
45. Quoted in Gay Edelman, "Will My Child Ever Have a Best Friend?," *ADDitude*. www.additudemag.com.
46. Mary Rooney, "ADHD in Teenagers," Child Mind Institute. https://childmind.org.
47. Carolyn Mallon, "Falling Through the Cracks: One ADHD Girl's Story," ADHD Homestead, April 29, 2015. http://adhdhome stead.net.
48. Marlene Snyder, "When Teens with ADHD Are Learning to Drive: Parent Strategies," October 14, 2016. www.great schools.org.
49. Jill Thijssen et al., "The Effectiveness of Parent Management Training—Oregon Model in Clinically Referred Children with Externalizing Behavior Problems in the Netherlands," *Child Psychiatry and Human Development*, February 2017. www .ncbi.nlm.nih.gov.
50. Linda J. Pfiffner and Lauren M. Haack, "Behavior Management for School-Aged Children with ADHD," *Child and Adolescent Psychiatric Clinics of North America*, 2014. www .ncbi.nlm.nih.gov.
51. Cristina Margolis, "My Daughter's Confession Crushed Me," *ADDitude*, Fall 2017. www.additudemag.com.
52. Quoted in Kerry King, Daleen Alexander, and Joseph Seabi, "Siblings' Perceptions of Their ADHD-Diagnosed Siblings' Impact on the Family System," *International Journal of Environmental Research and Public Health*, September 2016. www.ncbi.nlm.nih.gov.
53. Quoted in King, Alexander, and Seabi, "Siblings' Perceptions of Their ADHD-Diagnosed Siblings' Impact on the Family System."
54. Noreen Ryan and Tim McDougall, *Nursing Children and Young People with ADHD.* London: Routledge, 2009, p. 98.
55. Ryan and McDougall, *Nursing Children and Young People with ADHD*, p. 98.
56. Johan Wiklund, Holger Patzelt, and Dimo Dimov, "Entrepreneurship and Psychological Disorders: How ADHD Can Be Productively Harnessed," *Journal of Business Venturing Insights*, vol. 6, 2016, p. 17.
57. Quoted in Wiklund, Patzelt, and Dimov, "Entrepreneurship and Psychological Disorders," p. 17.

58. Quoted in *ADDitude* Editors, "What I Would Never Trade Away," *ADDitude*. www.additudemag.com.

Chapter 4: Can ADHD Be Treated or Cured?

59. National Institute of Neurological Disorders and Stroke, "Attention Deficit–Hyperactivity Disorder Information Page." www.ninds.nih.gov.
60. Alaa M. Hamed, Aaron J. Kauer, and Hanna E. Stevens, "Why the Diagnosis of Attention Deficit Hyperactivity Disorder Matters," *Frontiers in Psychiatry*, 2015. www.ncbi.nlm.nih.gov.
61. Charles Bradley, "The Behavior of Children Receiving Benzedrine," *American Journal of Psychiatry*, November 1937.
62. American Academy of Pediatrics, "Common ADHD Medications & Treatments for Children," January 10, 2017. www.healthychildren.org.
63. Thomas E. Brown, "Should My Child Take an ADHD Drug Holiday?," Understood. www.understood.org.
64. American Academy of Pediatrics, "Common ADHD Medications & Treatments for Children."
65. Richard Gallagher, Howard B. Abikoff, and Elana G. Spira, *Organizational Skills Training for Children with ADHD: An Empirically Supported Treatment*. New York: Guilford, 2014, p. 5.
66. American Academy of Pediatrics, "Behavior Therapy for Children with ADHD," January 9, 2017. www.healthychildren.org.
67. R.E.A. Loren et al., "Effects of an 8-Session Behavioral Parent Training Group for Parents of Children with ADHD on Child Impairment and Parenting Confidence," *Journal of Attention Disorders*, February 2015. www.ncbi.nlm.nih.gov.
68. David C. Agerter, "ADHD Diet: Do Food Additives Cause Hyperactivity?," Mayo Clinic, September 28, 2017. www.mayoclinic.org.
69. ClinicalTrials.gov, "Helping College Students with ADHD Lead Healthier Lifestyles," US National Library of Medicine. https://clinicaltrials.gov.
70. James John McGough et al., "Developmental Pilot Study of External Trigeminal Nerve Stimulation for ADHD," Grantome. http://grantome.com.
71. Centers for Disease Control and Prevention, "Attention-Deficit/Hyperactivity Disorder."

American Psychiatric Association
800 Maine Ave. SW, Suite 900
Washington, DC 20024
website: www.psychiatry.org

The American Psychiatric Association is a professional organization for psychiatrists, who are medical doctors who specialize in diagnosing and treating mental disorders. The website has information about ADHD, including symptoms, causes, diagnosis, treatment, and relevant research.

American Psychological Association
750 First St. NE
Washington, DC 20002-4242
website: www.apa.org

The American Psychological Association is a professional organization for psychologists, who are licensed to provide psychological therapy. Its website contains information about all aspects of ADHD, including symptoms, diagnosis, treatment, research, and more.

Centers for Disease Control and Prevention (CDC)
1600 Clifton Rd.
Atlanta, GA 30329
website: www.cdc.gov

The CDC is the US government agency responsible for protecting Americans from health and safety threats. It provides detailed information about all aspects of ADHD, including up-to-date statistics. The CDC also conducts research and shares its findings with the public.

Children and Adults with Attention-Deficit/ Hyperactivity Disorder (CHADD)

4601 Presidents Dr., Suite 300
Lanham, MD 20706
website: www.chadd.org

CHADD is also known as the National Resource Center on ADHD. It is funded by the CDC and serves as a membership organization that supports families affected by ADHD. Its website provides extensive information about all aspects of ADHD and offers links to other ADHD resources.

Mayo Clinic

200 First St. SW
Rochester, MN 55905
website: www.mayoclinic.org

The Mayo Clinic is a nonprofit organization that runs widely acclaimed hospitals and medical centers. Its website has detailed information about ADHD, including symptoms, diagnosis, treatment, and living with the disorder.

Medline Plus

US National Library of Medicine
8600 Rockville Pike
Bethesda, MD 20894
website: https://medlineplus.org

Medline Plus is a website produced by the National Library of Medicine. It contains detailed information about all aspects of ADHD, including symptoms, diagnosis, treatment, living with the disorder, and related research. It also offers articles for specific groups of people affected by ADHD, such as children, teenagers, parents, and women.

National Institute of Mental Health (NIMH)

6001 Executive Blvd., Room 6200, MSC9663
Bethesda, MD 20892-9663
website: www.nimh.nih.gov

The NIMH is a US government agency that is part of the National Institutes of Health, which performs research and educates the public about health issues and conditions. The NIMH website offers information on all aspects of ADHD, including symptoms, causes, diagnosis, treatment, and current research.

National Institute of Neurological Disorders and Stroke (NINDS)

PO Box 5810
Bethesda, MD 20824
website: www.ninds.nih.gov

NINDS is a government agency that is part of the National Institutes of Health. It sponsors and conducts research on ADHD and provides information to the public about all aspects of the disorder.

Psychology Today

115 E. Twenty-Third St., 9th Floor
New York, NY 10010
website: www.psychologytoday.com/basics/adhd

Psychology Today began as a magazine about mental health topics and has expanded to include a website with articles by experts. The ADHD section has articles about living with ADHD, advice for families, and information about diagnosis, treatment, causes, and relevant research.

Understood

website: www.understood.org

Understood is a nonprofit organization that supports families dealing with ADHD. It provides detailed information about all aspects of ADHD and offers access to expert advice and mutual support from individuals, parents, and families affected by ADHD.

For Further Research

Books

Nicole Horning, *Living with ADHD.* New York: Lucent, 2018.

Carla Mooney, *Teens and ADHD.* San Diego: ReferencePoint, 2017.

John Perritano, *ADHD and Other Behavior Disorders.* Broomall, PA: Mason Crest, 2017.

Whitney Sanderson, *Living with ADHD.* San Diego: Reference-Point, 2018.

Monique Vescia and Alvin Silverstein, *What You Can Do About ADHD.* New York: Enslow, 2015.

Internet Sources

Traci Angel, "Everything You Need to Know About ADHD," Healthline, July 13, 2017. www.healthline.com/health/adhd.

Denise Foley, "ADHD & Kids: The Truth About Attention Deficit Hyperactivity Disorder," Time.com. http://time.com/growing-up -with-adhd.

Richard A. Friedman, "A Natural Fix for A.D.H.D.," *New York Times*, October 31, 2014. www.nytimes.com/2014/11/02/opin ion/sunday/a-natural-fix-for-adhd.html.

Medical News Today Editorial Team, "ADD/ADHD: Causes, Symptoms, and Research," Medical News Today, January 5, 2016. www.medicalnewstoday.com/info/adhd.

TeensHealth, "ADHD." https://kidshealth.org/en/teens/adhd.html ?WT.ac=ctg#catlearning.

WebMD, "Understanding ADHD—the Basics." www.webmd.com /add-adhd/childhood-adhd/understanding-adhd-basics.

Index

Note: Boldface page numbers indicate illustrations.

Picture Credits

Cover: MonkeyBusiness/Depositphotos